How to Remember Everything in the New Testament and General Conference

How to Remember Everything in the New Testament and General Conference

By David R. Larsen
with
Brett D. Benson

ISBN: 1-978-155517-997-7
ISBN: 1-55517-997-5

Published by Cedar Fort, Inc.
2474 W. 700 S., Springville, Utah, 84663
www.cedarfort.com
Distributed by Cedar Fort

Library of Congress Cataloging-in-Publication Data

Larsen, David R.
How to remember anything in the New Testament and general conference / David R. Larsen with Brett D. Benson.
p. cm.
ISBN-13: 978-1-55517-997-7
1. Bible. N.T.—Mnemonic devices. 2. Bible. N.T.—Study and teaching. 3. Church of Jesus Christ of Latter-day Saints—Doctrines—Study and teaching. 4. Mormon Church—Doctrines—Study and teaching. 5. Mnemonics. I. Benson, Brett D. II. Title.

BS617.7.L37 2006
153.1'4088289332—dc22

2006032354

Cover design by Nicole Williams
Edited and typeset by Kimiko M. Hammari

Printed in the United States of America
10 9 8 7 6 5 4 3 2 1

Printed on acid-free paper

CONTENTS

ACKNOWLEDGMENTS

You will note there have been two of us working on this edition. My partner and bishop, Brett Benson, is a seminary principal and an excellent teacher. Brett is the primary author of chapter 10 on teaching but has also contributed invaluable insights, supporting scriptures, and other ideas along the way. Most of this book is written in the first person—"I" being David Larsen. If there are errors, I am responsible. Most of the principles and methods for remembering are my contributions, although precious few are original to me. Many of the other great illustrations have come from Bishop Benson and others to whom I am indebted.

Of special note are the contributions on memorizing in chapter 8, from my good friend John Piatt, who not only memorized the entire Sermon on the Mount but lives it. I would like to also thank my former bishop, Jay Pimentel, now Public Affairs Director for the Church in the Oakland Bay area, who provided the initial quote from President Kimball and opened my eyes to the value of the A RECORD formula in teaching the gospel to others.

I would especially like to thank my friend Ron Nybo for his many hours spent proofreading, as well as his super suggestions and encouraging words. Although I feel the A RECORD formula, which is really the heart of the book, came by inspiration, the nudge to seek that inspiration for a better, easier-to-remember acronym came from Ron.

Also a special thanks goes to the editors at Cedar Fort, Heather Holm and Kimiko Hammari, who ended up having to do more work than they should have, to make my original ramblings more readable. And to my wife, Maureen, for her tolerance, patience, and proofreading into the wee hours of the night.

Finally I would like to thank my dear parents, Howard and Josephine, who instilled in me a love for learning, especially for the scriptures. I don't think enough parents realize the great impact their teachings and examples will have on their children. Both of my parents studied and often quoted scriptures. Their example has been of tremendous value to my siblings and me in not only guiding our lives but in teaching our children as well. And as an extension of my parents, I wish to give thanks and pay tribute to the many teachers I've had over the years who have strived to help me better understand the scriptures. The ripples of their careful preparation and edification continue into eternity.

INTRODUCTION

The Apostle Paul wrote that "perilous times shall come" (2 Timothy 3:1). Now we see that they are here! Actually, they have been in every dispensation. But it appears that the forces of good and evil are rallying their troops for the final battle. One of my favorite quotes in this regard, that you will see again in chapter 1, is from Elder Marion G. Romney who observed that "the great over-all struggle in the world today is, as it has always been, for the souls of men. Every soul is personally engaged in the struggle, and *he makes the fight with what is in his mind*" (Conference Report, April 1960; emphasis added). It is my great hope that this work will, in some significant way, better enable you to "treasure up in your mind" (D&C 84:85) and in your children and students the words of eternal life. If you apply the principles contained herein, I'm confident you and they will be better prepared and more easily able to draw upon the word of God in your days of trial, to deal with whatever challenges might lie ahead, with wisdom, faith, and courage.

For Readers of the First Edition

If you were fortunate enough to purchase my first book in this series, *How to Remember Everything in the Old Testament*, you will see some similarities in this book, as this is patterned on the first book. Chapters 1, 2, and 10 are completely new. Chapters 3, 8, and 12, except for minor changes, are the same as before. Chapters 8 and 12 already had illustrations from the New Testament, so they actually seemed more appropriate here than in the first book. Chapter 3 has some basic introductory information about the nature of memory that hasn't changed. All the remaining chapters contain principles and methods mentioned previously but with significant additions, adaptations, or alterations.

Since repetition is the mother of memory, I hope you will find the review helpful to reinforce concepts previously learned. I believe you will find the new information and adaptations for remembering conference addresses, creating memory mapping, and teaching to be well worth the added investment.

1

REMEMBERING—THE FORGOTTEN KEY TO RIGHTEOUSNESS IN THE NEW TESTAMENT

Spencer W. Kimball once observed: "When you look in the dictionary for the most important word, do you know what it is? It could be 'remember.'" He went on to note that all members of The Church of Jesus Christ of Latter-day Saints have made covenants. We've been taught what to do and how to do it, but "our greatest need is to remember." That is why everyone goes to sacrament meeting every Sabbath day—to take the sacrament and listen to the priests pray that they "may always remember him and keep his commandments which he has given them."[1]

Jesus gave us a perfect example by remembering and showing obedience to the will of His father (see John 8:28–29). When He was tempted by Satan, He responded by quoting the Old Testament: "It is written, Man shall not live by bread alone, but by every word that proceedeth out of the mouth of God" (Matthew 4:4). We know from Lehi's dream that the "word of God" is as an iron rod, which if firmly grasped, can lead us successfully through the mists of darkness and the trials and temptations of mortality (1 Nephi 8:19–24). Yet how on earth can we expect to hold fast to and follow the counsel of God if we can't remember what it was?

Jesus invites "all ye that labour and are heavy laden" to "learn of [him] . . . and ye shall find rest unto your souls" (Matthew 11:28–29). Accordingly, we are taught that in times of quandary, or indecision, it's a good idea to ask ourselves, "What would Jesus do?" But again, how can we answer that question, how can we follow His example, if we cannot remember what he said and did—what we have learned of Him?[2]

One of the primary purposes of this book, therefore, is to help readers learn how to more effectively remember the actions and responses, as well as the attributes and teachings of Jesus Christ and His apostles, particularly as recorded in the New Testament but also in our day. As we are told in the Doctrine and Covenants, regarding the words of Christ, "whether by mine own voice or by the voice of my servants, it is the same" (1:38). In future chapters when you see reference to "the scriptures," keep in mind that this includes inspired utterances from modern apostles and prophets as well.

In Order to Win the War

While serving as a chaplain for the Navy and Marine Corps, I participated in exercises that cost millions of dollars to help prepare our troops for war. No doubt these preparations were vital to the survival of our brave men and women in combat. However, President Ezra Taft Benson observed, "Some of the greatest battles we will face will be fought within the silent chambers of our own souls."[3] Elder Jeffrey R. Holland referred to the same struggles when he spoke of "those who endure conflicts fought in the lonely foxholes of the heart."[4] Elder Marion G. Romney provided additional insights into the nature of these battles and what we need to win. He noted:

> The great over-all struggle in the world today is, as it has always been, for the souls of men. Every soul is personally engaged in the struggle, and *he makes the fight with what is in his mind.* In the final analysis, the battleground is, for each individual, within himself. Inevitably he gravitates towards the subjects of his thoughts. . . . If we would escape the lusts of the flesh and build for ourselves and for our children great and noble characters, we must *keep in our minds and in their minds* true and righteous principles for our thoughts and their thoughts to dwell upon."[5] (emphasis added)

How do we keep these true and righteous principles in our minds? Obviously through our memory—by remembering what we have read or have been taught.

What Behavioral Scientists Have Learned

President Benson, Elder Holland, and Elder Romney each show awareness of an important principle that psychologists and psychiatrists, though somewhat reticent to recognize initially, have now accepted as one of the greatest behavioral science discoveries of the twentieth century. Prior to the 1970s, there was a lot of speculation and theories as to the dominant determinants of behavior and emotions. Of course, there is still speculation on the details. However, in the mid 1970s, several different groups of behavioral scientists discovered through careful, independent, empirical analysis the primary determinant of our feelings, actions, and reactions. They noted this key factor was not what went on around us, not so much how our parents treated us, or the events in our environments (although these all are important). No, the primary cause is what goes on *inside* our heads—how we interpret what happens to us, the meaning we give to events, what we choose or allow ourselves to believe and think about most of the time. In short, the primary determinants of our feelings and behavior were found to be our dominant thoughts.[6]

The quality of these thoughts, beliefs, and interpretations, however, are pretty much limited to and dependent upon what we remember. If, for example, someone makes a statement that we take offense to and all we can think of is how unfair, false, or insulting that was, we are likely to feel hurt and angry. If the only way we can think to respond is to follow our gut instincts (or some approach we have recently seen on TV, like "I don't have to take this from you"), then we will likely retaliate and say or do something that would be offensive to them in return. However, if at that moment in time we are able to recall relevant examples and counsel from Christ, we will likely not strike back but rather resist those "natural" inclinations to retaliate and go to the offender in private and seek reconciliation (see Matthew 5:22–25; 39, 44; 18:15; D&C 42:88).

Perhaps that is why the apostle Paul counseled the Philippians, "Finally, brethren, whatsoever things are true, whatsoever things are honest, whatsoever things are just, whatsoever things are pure, whatsoever things are lovely, whatsoever things are of good report; if there be any virtue, and if there be any praise, *think on these things*" (4:8–9; emphasis added). The Lord reiterated to the early saints in this dispensation: "Treasure up in your minds continually the words of life, and it shall be given you in the very hour that portion that shall be meted unto every man" (D&C 84:85); and "let virtue garnish thy thoughts unceasingly; then shall thy confidence wax strong in the presence of God" (D&C 121:45).

Other Scriptures Testify of Its Importance

It's no wonder then that the admonition to "remember" is one of the most oft repeated directives in scripture. In the book of Deuteronomy, God commanded Israel no less than seven times to "remember" or "not forget" their God as well as His counsel and commandments. Through Moses, He said, "Take heed to thyself, and keep thy soul diligently, lest thou *forget* the things which thine eyes have seen, and lest they depart from thy heart all the days of thy life" (Deuteronomy 4:9; emphasis added). "And thou shalt teach them diligently unto thy children, and shalt talk of them when thou sittest in thine house, and when thou walkest by the way, and when thou liest down, and when thou risest up" (6:7). Why? So they would not forget.

Sadly, we now see that these commandments to remember were all warranted, because Israel did forget. As their judges and King David later lamented, "Our fathers understood not thy wonders in Egypt; they *remembered not* the multitude of thy mercies; but provoked him" (Psalms 106:7; emphasis added). As a result, we know most turned from their God and Savior and, because of their forgetfulness and resulting unfaithfulness, were made to wander in the desert forty years, and later were conquered and carried off into Babylon. Yet it's plain to see, one of the primary reasons for their fall into apostasy and perpetual problems was that they simply did not follow this commandment to "remember, and not forget."

No doubt Jesus was well aware of the importance of remembering. Perhaps it was for this reason, as well as others, that He promised to send the people a special assistant to aid them in this important task of remembering. He called it the "Comforter, which is the Holy Ghost, whom the Father will send in my name," and explained that "he shall teach you all things, and bring all things to your remembrance, whatsoever I have said unto you" (John 14:26). We will talk more about this special agent of memory in the next chapter. As we'll see, there is much that He can do to assist us in the learning process, especially in learning and remembering scriptures, if we will seek and qualify ourselves for this blessing.

In the later record and epistles of Jesus' apostles, the admonition to "remember" or "not forget" is repeated no less than a dozen times.[7] For example, Paul, after warning those in Ephesus that deceivers would enter in among them "not sparing the flock," cautioned, "Therefore watch, and *remember*, that by the space of three years I ceased not to warn every one night and day with tears" (Acts 20:31; emphasis added). Since our church leaders cannot always be with us, it's imperative that we learn to remember their counsel, that we might be able to stand firm when we encounter men speaking perverse things to try and draw us away from the truth.

Paul praised the Corinthians for remembering in the context of following Christ's example. Paul said, "Be ye followers of me, even as I also am of Christ. Now I praise you, brethren, that ye *remember* me in all things, and keep the ordinances, as I delivered them to you" (1 Corinthians 11:1–2; emphasis added). As noted above, we can hardly follow an example if we can't remember what was said or done. And of course, "keeping ordinances" also requires remembering.

Later the apostle Paul equated remembering with righteousness when he said:

> For God is not unrighteous, therefore he will *not forget* your work and labor of love, which ye have showed toward his name, in that ye have ministered to the saints, and do minister. And we desire that every one of you do show the same diligence to the full assurance of hope unto the end. (JST Hebrews 6:10–11; emphasis added)

Does that imply that if we forget his work and words then we are not being righteous?

The Cycle to Remember

I was in the process of writing this book when the April 2006 conference was broadcast. I was interested to hear Elder Bednar note that along with contention and rudeness, one of the other things that can cause us to lose the direction of the Spirit is being "forgetful" (see Alma 37:41, 43). Moreover, this pattern appears to be cyclical, or characteristic of a syndrome. The more we remember the Lord and His counsel and keep His commandments, the more likely it is that we will have His Spirit to be with us. And the more of His influence that we have in our lives and in our studies, the more likely we will be to find and remember that which will be of greatest importance to us.

On the other hand, the less we remember Jesus, the less likely we are to keep His commandments. The less we remember Him and keep His commandments, the less likely we will be to have His Spirit and the influence of the Holy Ghost in our lives. And the less we experience this influence in our lives, the less we will remember of the things of the Lord.

Jesus said, regarding knowledge of the mysteries of the kingdom, "For whosoever receiveth, to him shall be given, and he shall have more abundance: but whosoever continueth not to receive, from him shall be taken away even that he hath" (JST Matthew 13:12; see also 2 Nephi 28:29–30). In this dispensation, the Lord reiterated this idea in the very first section of the Doctrine and Covenants when he spoke to the man who repents not: "From him shall be taken even the light which he has received; for my Spirit shall not always strive with man, sayeth the Lord of Hosts" (D&C 1:33; see also 60:3).

It's Up to Us

You will note that this is not a capricious withdrawal of spirit and light; rather it is dependent upon our exercise of our agency. We cannot control when the Spirit comes. As Jesus noted, it's like the wind (see John 3:8). However, we do have control over what we choose to receive, remember, and apply. And I believe that this is the idea: the less we forget and the more we apply the counsel of the Lord, the more we remember His teachings, the more we "treasure up" in our minds and incorporate into our lives, the more we will receive and the better we will be able to remember and apply it. Isn't that the cycle of eternal progression?

We can see this pattern carried out in every book of scripture. I believe that is why God, through Moses, commanded the Israelites more than a dozen times to remember, or not forget, what they had been taught. He knew that if they did forget, they would lose what they had and fall. Unfortunately, that is what happened. The Israelites did forget, and when they forgot, they stopped seeking and receiving, and then they lost the light and knowledge they had. It wasn't long before they fell. The same pattern, of course, is manifest in the Book of Mormon, both before and after the visit of Jesus Christ to the Americas. And the same process followed the preaching of Jesus and His apostles in the New Testament.

The Way Back

So, if forgetting leads to apostasy or a fall, what is the way back? The Lord, speaking prophetically through Ezekiel of the outcasts of Israel, answers that question: "And they that escape of you shall *remember me* among the nations whither they shall be carried captives" (Ezekiel 6:9; emphasis added). It is apparently this act of remembering the Lord and His mercy, His counsel, our covenants and promises, that lead to the repentance process and help us return to the favor of the Lord.

The Lord reiterates this process in speaking to the saints under condemnation in this dispensation: "And they shall remain under this condemnation until they repent and *remember* the new covenant, even the Book of Mormon and the former commandments which I have given them, not only to say, but to do according to that which I have written" (D&C 84:57; emphasis added).

And so it is, that while forgetting the word of God can lead to our downfall, remembering appears to be a key to salvation.

In Conclusion

Knowing the importance placed on remembering in the scriptures, and how important it is to remember the Savior, His teachings, and His example; and realizing how we conduct our lives is largely a result of what we can readily recall from memory, it appears imperative that we do the following.

1. Learn how to "treasure up" in our minds and memory the words of Christ and His inspired apostles, prophets, and other church leaders in our day.
2. Follow God's admonition to teach these things to our children (see Deuteronomy 6:7), and do so in such a way that they will not forget to whom they must look for guidance and salvation.
3. Continue to work on improving our memories for the scriptures so that we might be more effective in sharing the principles of the gospel with others in classroom or missionary settings. If we want to teach these truths to others, we must first treasure them up in our own minds (see D&C 84:85).

That is what this book is designed to help us do—treasure up the truths of the gospel, particularly from the New Testament and general conference in such a way that we will easily remember these truths when needed.

Notes

(See "Sources" in the back for more complete references.)

1. "Circles of Exaltation" (address delivered at seminary and institute summer school, Brigham Young University, 28 June 1968), quoted in *Duties and Blessings of the Priesthood, Basic Manual for Priesthood Holders, Part B* (rev. 2000) Lesson 32, p. 268 (also quoted in earlier edition of same manual on page 272).
2. An observation made to the author by Bishop Barnard Madsen, March 15, 2006.
3. Ezra Taft Benson, "In His Steps," *Ensign*, Sept. 1988, 2.
4. Jeffrey R. Holland, "Broken Things to Mend," *Ensign*, May 2006, 69.
5. Marion G. Romney, Conference Report, April 1960, 111.

6. Aaron T. Beck, A. J. Rush, B. F. Shaw, and G. Emery, Cognitive Therapy of Depression; V.F. Guidano and G. Liotti, Cognitive Processes and Emotional Disorders.

7. Acts 20:31; 1 Corinthians 11:2; Galations 2:10; Ephesians 2:11; Colossians 4:18; 1 Thessalonians 2:9; 2 Thessalonians 2:5; Hebrews 6:10; 13:2,3, 16; Jude 1:17; Revelation 2:5; 3:3.

2

LEARNING BY THE SPIRIT

Generally when we think of receiving divine assistance in relation to remembering, we think of Jesus' promise recorded in John, that the Holy Ghost will bring all things, particularly Christ's words, to our "remembrance" (see John 14:26). As noted in chapter one, that would also include the words of his inspired servants. Various church leaders through the years have expounded on this promise. Elder Spencer W. Kimball taught, "The Holy Ghost is a revelator. . . . He is a reminder and will bring to our remembrance the things which we have learned and which we need in the time thereof."[1]

Elder James E. Talmage observed, "Through the influence of the Holy Spirit the powers of the human mind can be quickened and increased so that things past may be brought to remembrance."[2] (Quickened in this context means stimulated, roused, or invigorated.)

A Divine Study Guide

We know the Holy Ghost can help us remember, but I would like to suggest that we first focus on inviting the Spirit to assist us up front in this process of finding and storing knowledge. Jesus told his disciples, "The Comforter, which is the Holy Ghost, whom the Father will send in my name, he shall teach you all things" (John 14: 26). Moreover, He taught that if we seek Him, this Spirit is able to "guide [us] into all truth" (John 16:13).

Elder David A. Bednar opened his April 2006 conference address with the following prayer and invitation: "I pray for and invite the Holy Ghost to now assist me and you as we learn together."[3] This seems like a fitting model and the best way to begin any learning experience. Elder Bednar then taught:

> Taking "the Holy Spirit for [our] guide" (D&C 45:57) is possible and is essential for our spiritual growth and survival in an increasingly wicked world. Sometimes as Latter-day Saints we talk and act as though recognizing the influence of the Holy Ghost in our lives is the rare or exceptional event. We should remember, however, that the covenant promise is *that we may always have His Spirit to be with us.* This supernal blessing applies to every single member of the Church who has been baptized, confirmed, and instructed to "receive the Holy Ghost."[4] [emphasis in original]

Along with his mission to "guide us," this divine emissary from the Father can also lead us into a greater awareness of those things that would be most important for us to know and remember. As we read the scriptures, some things will be more relevant for us than others, as when Joseph Smith was reading the book of James. When he came across verse 5 of chapter 1, you will recall he had a very memorable experience. As he later recorded, "Never did any passage of scripture come with more power to the heart of man than this did at this time to mine. It seemed to enter with great force into every feeling of my heart."[5] It's apparent from this description that it was the Spirit of God that impressed that verse upon young Joseph's heart.

Many people can bear testimony to the power of the Spirit helping them to find and focus on scriptures relevant to their needs. It seems wise, therefore, to pray for the Spirit's assistance at the beginning of each scripture study session.

To Increase Our Understanding

The scriptures and latter-day church leaders also teach that the Holy Ghost can help us to better understand the important things we study. Three out of four of our scriptures are about an ancient people in a foreign land, translated into an older form of English from their ancient languages. As a result, the scriptures are not always easy to comprehend. Commentaries and footnotes are helpful in this regard, but the Holy Ghost is more effective.

For example, some people find the book of Isaiah in the Old Testament somewhat hard to comprehend, and therefore, hard to remember. However, Nephi noted that the words of Isaiah are plain to those with the spirit of prophecy—a gift of the Holy Ghost (see 2 Nephi 25:4). In other words, when we have the Spirit with us as we study, it is easier to understand what we read and therefore easier to store and remember this information.

Brigham Young noted, "The Holy Ghost reveals unto you things past, present, and to come; it makes your minds quick and vivid to understand the handiwork of the Lord."[6]

The Spirit can not only open the eyes of our understanding, but it can also enlighten the landscape of our consciousness to allow insights and an awareness of relationships that would otherwise go unnoticed. I still recall one of the first times this happened to me. I was seventeen years old working on my uncle's ranch for the summer. My cousin had been asked to give a talk in church, but she was kind enough to invite me to give the talk for her. I was dumb enough to accept. The weather had slowed down the farm work, so while I waited for the hay to dry, I took the opportunity to really get into the scriptures and seek answers to questions I'd been pondering. I recall one evening, sitting in a large sofa chair reading *Answers to Gospel Questions* by Joseph Fielding Smith. As I read and took notes, gradually and then somewhat suddenly the landscape of my understanding was illuminated, and I was able to see and understand concepts and connections in ways I had not previously imagined. It was literally like a light went on in my head and the "eyes of my understanding were opened" (D&C 110:1). Such is a gift of the Holy Ghost. As the apostle Paul said, "The natural man receiveth not the things of the Spirit . . . because they are spiritually discerned" (1 Corinthians 2:14). Although we might not normally even see, let alone understand such things, with the aid of the Spirit, that increased awareness and divine understanding can be ours.

Pondering Enhances Understanding

Pondering also helps to enhance understanding. When we read the scriptures and just try to "get through" our quota of pages for the day, we often do not take the time needed to ponder. As a result, we may not receive the insights our Father in Heaven might like to bless us with, and could bless us with, if we would just be still and ponder the words we read.

In his April 2006 conference address, Elder Henry B. Eyring told of a time when critical answers came to him after much pondering and prayer:

> I learned from that experience and countless repetitions that the description of the Holy Ghost

> as a still, small voice is real. It is poetic, but it is not poetry. Only when my heart has been still and quiet, in submission like a little child, has the Spirit been clearly audible to my heart and mind.[7]

In that same conference, Elder Bednar added a further description of the whisperings of the Spirit: "The influence of the Holy Ghost is described in the scriptures as 'a still small voice . . .' a 'voice of perfect mildness.' Thus, the Spirit of the Lord usually communicates with us in ways that are quiet, delicate, and subtle."[8]

Pondering as we read the scriptures can provide the "still and quiet" time needed to receive this "delicate and subtle" communication. But we must take the time and do it. And as Elder Eyring added in that same address, we must do so with a humble heart and a willingness to yield to the enticing of the Spirit. We must submit to the will of our Father in Heaven and follow the Savior in serving our fellowmen.

Guidance from the Spirit Should Not Be a Rare Experience

Now, of course, we are not always going to receive dramatic guidance from the Spirit when we ponder, pray, and study. However, as Elder Bednar noted above, "the covenant promise is *that we may always have His Spirit to be with us.*" In Doctrine and Covenants 121 (cited in chapter 1), after the admonition to "let virtue garnish thy thoughts unceasing," the Lord declared, "The Holy Ghost shall be thy constant companion, and thy scepter an unchanging scepter of righteousness and truth" (v. 46). These two scriptures suggest to me that if we are living right, this divine guidance and insight should not be a rare occurrence for latter-day saints.

Moreover, what we are talking about here—how to receive guidance from the Spirit—is not peripheral to the gospel. It's core central and no doubt the most important principle in this book. As the following experiences from Brigham Young and Wilford

Woodruff illustrate, it is critical to our ultimate success during this period of mortal probation.

On February 23, 1847, Brigham Young recorded the following vision and message from the then deceased prophet Joseph Smith.

> Tell the people to be humble and faithful, and be sure to keep the Spirit of the Lord and it will lead them right. Be careful and not turn away the still small voice; it will teach them what to do and where to go; it will yield the fruits of the kingdom. Tell the [people] to keep their hearts open to conviction, so that when the Holy Ghost comes to them, their hearts will be ready to receive it. They can tell the Spirit of the Lord from all other spirits; it will whisper peace and joy to their souls; it will take malice, hatred, strife and all evil from their hearts; and their whole desire will be to do good, bring forth righteousness and build up the kingdom of God. Tell the [people] if they will follow the spirit of the Lord they will go right."[9]

Recently I was surprised to see a similar quote from a visitation of Brigham Young to Wilford Woodruff in 1880, while Woodruff was president of the Church. (Brigham Young died in 1877.) During their brief visit, Brigham Young told Wilford Woodruff:

> I want you to teach the people—and I want you to follow this counsel yourself—that they must labor and so live as to obtain the Holy Spirit, for without this you cannot build up the kingdom; without the Spirit of God you are in danger of walking in the dark, and in danger of failing to accomplish your calling as apostles and as Elders in the church and kingdom of God.[10]

Joseph Smith's counsel to Brigham Young came from the book *Alive in Christ* by Robert L. Millet, who was at the time

Dean of Religion at Brigham Young University. In the epilogue to his book and just before this quote, Millet notes:

> Thus one of the most important labors we can perform is to seek the Spirit. The older I get and the more I reflect upon the truths of the gospel, the more I am driven toward this one imperative: Seek the Spirit. If eternal life is indeed the greatest of all the gifts of God in eternity (D&C 6:13; 14:7), then surely the companionship of the Holy Ghost is the greatest gift we can receive in time, in this mortal sphere. (*Discourses of Wilford Woodruff,* 5)[11]

Note Impressions from the Spirit

Since promptings from the Spirit are of such great worth, it's probably wise to jot down these impressions as they come during scripture study and pondering. Someone once said, "The shortest pencil is better than the longest memory." In truth, each have their place. But often these precious impressions from the "still small voice" are fleeting, and if we don't gaff them with a bit of ink or lead, we may forget them.

While I was on my mission in Argentina, Elder Bernard P. Brockbank, who was at the time a member of the Quorum of Seventy, stopped by to visit with the missionaries. On that occasion, he shared with us his system for remembering the promptings of the Spirit. He told us that when he said his prayers, he often did so with a pencil in hand and a pad of paper in order to write down his impressions.

I remember thinking, "What a novel idea!" I don't think this practice had even occurred to most of us before. People don't usually pray with a pen and paper in hand. But if we really believe Heavenly Father can hear and answer our prayers, it makes sense to do so. Moreover, this note-taking will further enable us to reflect on these impressions and take time to commit them to memory. At the very least, writing down these bits of insight and inspiration, and reading them over, will help us to better remember, retain, and apply them in our lives.

The Spirit Can Assist in Storing Knowledge

One of the most important keys to ready recall is effective storage. In other words, we must be able to effectively "treasure up" in our memory those things that are most important for us to remember so that they can be easily retrieved in our hour of need. Various functions of the Spirit seem tailored to this process. For example, as Brigham Young and others have noted, the Spirit can "quicken" our minds, enabling us to think and respond faster and more effectively, thus facilitating the comprehension and retention of information.

Regarding this special ability and learning in general, Orson Pratt noted:

> We need the help of the Lord, in some measure, in our researches, to learn anything; we need the influence of the Spirit of God to quicken the light that is within us, for light cleaves to light, and the Spirit of God is light, and it cleaves unto the light that enters into the composition of the spirit of man; and when we keep his commandments the Lord is ever ready and willing to quicken the judgment, inform the mind, and lead us along in our thinking and reflecting powers."[12]

There is an interesting idea regarding gospel learning, which suggests that from an eternal perspective, we don't really learn anything new on earth, at least not gospel knowledge. We have been taught all these concepts before in our pre-mortal experience. Therefore, much of our gospel learning here on earth is simply relearning, or as Elder Pratt suggests, "light cleav[ing] to light." If we equate light to knowledge or truth, then it makes sense to say, as memory researchers have found, that knowledge or new information is more easily captured and stored in memory when it is associated, paired, or in some other way connected with something we have already learned, even if we have "forgotten" or cannot recall that previous learning. Moreover, the Spirit seems to be a catalyst for making those connections and restoring those recollections, at least of gospel knowledge, and perhaps other knowledge as well.

This phenomena occurred with my wife when she received the discussions from the missionaries. At the time, she was in her early teens attending a Catholic school in England. But when she was taught the lessons, she had no problem understanding and accepting the doctrine, particularly regarding God (that God is our Father in Heaven, a glorified man, and that the Father, Son, and Holy Ghost are three distinct persons). This, of course, was not the orthodox Catholic doctrine, nor was it ever discussed, that she could recall, by her parents, guardians, or previous teachers. Nevertheless, she found these "new" teachings congruent with her deepest understanding. In discussing this concept with the missionaries, it was thought that perhaps this was a recollection of a pre-mortal memory. However, some years later an aunt reminded her that when she was less than four years of age, a pair of LDS missionaries lived next door to them. According to the aunt, they used to practice their discussions with her. Perhaps she was the only one in the village who would listen. Now, whether or not my wife's initial knowledge came from these early missionaries or was a carry-over from her pre-mortal education, once she heard the message again, as the missionaries taught and bore witness by the Spirit, it resonated within her and she immediately recognized it to be true.

Of course, Elder Pratt's other potent points are that "we need the help of the Lord . . . in our researches, to learn anything" and when we keep his commandments the Lord is ever ready and willing to enhance our mental faculties to improve our judgment, teach us, and "lead us along in our thinking," all of which can assist us in storing up treasures of knowledge. Most members of the Church can attest to the ability of the Spirit to "impress things upon our mind" and into memory with such power that they are not soon forgotten.

The Spirit Can Assist in Relating to What We Read

The Spirit can also help us to relate to or identify with the characters we read about and develop a measure of empathy for them. This can aid us in not only understanding intellectually but emotionally as well and further facilitate retention. In chapter 5, you will learn how emotions can enhance memories. Although I am not aware of any scripture that directly states this, I know the Spirit can also help us to feel what the characters we read about might have felt and to feel the power of their words. As a result, their message will be more deeply impressed upon our hearts as well as our minds. I know this to be true because I have experienced it. Perhaps you have as well.

Recently, during a period of fasting, I decided to reread the story of Joseph and his reunion with his brothers in Genesis chapters 42–46. As I was doing so, I found it easy to empathize with Joseph, to imagine what he must have felt upon seeing his brothers after so many years. Even though they had been cruel to him, he still loved them and longed to see them once again. I could not only imagine but could also feel what he must have felt when he saw how the hearts of his brothers had changed and the love and concern they now showed for their father. How it must have touched him when he saw how their hearts had mellowed over the years. Finally, I could feel at least a portion of what Joseph must have felt when he witnessed their willingness now to not only protect but even be imprisoned themselves in the place of their younger brother. What joy and rejoicing he must have felt, like a father whose prodigal son has returned. Indeed the events of chapter 45 are so touching that I could not help but weep even before I read of Joseph's cries. Such feelings are not soon forgotten, nor are the recorded events that evoke them.

To Be Worthy of the Spirit in Our Lives

All people baptized into the Church have been given the gift of the Holy Ghost. But how often do we "receive" it and rely on its promptings to help us remember? Joseph Fielding Smith stated:

> It is my judgment that there are many members of this Church who have . . . had hands laid upon their heads for the gift of the Holy Ghost, who have never received that gift, that is the manifestations of it. Why? Because they have never put themselves in order to receive these manifestations. They have never humbled themselves. They have never taken the steps that would prepare them for the companionship of the Holy Ghost."[13]

So what are those steps? According to then Elder Smith, humility is one of the qualities necessary to receive assistance from the Spirit. This seems to coincide with the admonitions of Solomon and Isaiah who taught, "Be not wise in thine own eyes" (Proverbs 3:7; see also Isaiah 5:21), for those who think they know enough shall not be given more. In fact, they may lose what they have. Some mistakenly equate humility with weakness, but a better biblical definition is a willingness to heed and learn.

In another sermon, Joseph Fielding Smith taught how we receive the gift of the Holy Ghost: "The Holy Ghost will not dwell with that person who is unwilling to obey and keep the commandments of God or who violates those commandments willingly. . . . That great gift comes to us only through humility and faith and obedience."[14] His words remind me of the teachings in Doctrine and Covenants 93:28: "He that keepeth his commandments receiveth truth and light, until he is glorified in truth and knoweth all things."

Humility, faith, and obedience appear then to be important keys to activating this gift. But, like any gift of God, we must ask for and seek it. Jesus invited us to "ask, and it shall be given you; seek, and ye shall find; knock, and it shall be opened unto you" (Matthew 7:7–8). To His disciples in America, He promised: "And whatsoever ye shall ask the Father in my name, which is right, believing that ye shall receive, behold it shall be given unto you" (3 Nephi 18:20).

Finally, having sought this gift, as Jesus counseled, we must be open, receptive, and responsive to its influence when it comes. Otherwise, it will not abide with us (Mormon 2:26).

I wonder if one of the problems here might not be that most of us simply don't believe the Holy Ghost can or will help us with our memory challenges. But if remembering really is important for our salvation, as noted in chapter 1, then why wouldn't He? Perhaps the thought is that most of us feel our memory challenges are just too mundane for Him. And maybe many of them are. But remembering the word of the Lord and scriptures is very much in line with what Jesus declared his role to be. However, it does seem to require faith on our part.

This reminds me of Alma's counsel regarding the cultivation of faith in Alma 32. I suggest you read that chapter again with this gift of the Spirit in mind and conduct a little "experiment upon [His] words. . . . Give place for a portion of [His] words." Plant this seed of faith in your heart. "If ye do not cast it out by your unbelief, that ye will resist the Spirit of the Lord, behold it will begin to swell within your breasts; . . . [and] to enlighten [your] understanding" (v. 27–28).

Avoid Withdrawals from the Spirit

Elder Bednar counseled that we should also endeavor to discern when we "withdraw [ourselves] from the Spirit of the Lord, that it may have no place in [us] to guide [us] in wisdom's paths that [we] may be blessed, prospered, and preserved" (Mosiah 2:36).[15] He further explained that the pointers in the Liahona (symbolic of the Holy Ghost) operated "according to the faith and diligence and heed" (1 Nephi 16:28) of the travelers. Therefore, whenever we entertain doubts, or are not diligent in heeding his promptings, we withdraw ourselves from the assistance we could otherwise receive from the Spirit. Elder Bednar also mentioned, as noted in chapter 1, that the Liahona failed to work when family members were contentious, rude, slothful, or forgetful (see 1 Nephi 18:12, 21; Alma 37:41, 43).

Elder Eyring, commenting on a similar theme (how we can avoid sin and retain the Spirit and our blessings), quoted King Benjamin's counsel:

> But this much I can tell you, that if ye do not watch yourselves, and your thoughts, and your words, and your deeds, and observe the commandments of God, and continue in the faith of what ye have heard concerning the coming of our Lord, even unto the end of your lives, ye must perish. And now, O man, *remember*, and perish not."
>
> With the help of the Holy Ghost, we can watch over ourselves. We can pray to recognize and reject the first thoughts of sin. . . . And we can, when we must, pray for the humility and the faith to repent."[16] (emphasis added)

All these things will, of course, help us to retain the companionship the Spirit.

In his concluding remarks on receiving the Spirit, Elder Bednar, stated:

> The Spirit of the Lord can be our guide and will bless us with direction, instruction, and spiritual protection during our mortal journey. We invite the Holy Ghost into our lives through meaningful personal and family prayer, feasting upon the words of Christ, diligent and exacting obedience, faithfulness and honoring of covenants, and through virtue, humility, and service. And we steadfastly should avoid things that are immodest, coarse, crude, sinful, or evil that cause us to withdraw ourselves from the Holy Ghost.[17]

In Conclusion

All of the above can be boiled down to a few simple recommendations. If we want to be led in learning the most important things for us, if we want increased understanding, comprehension, and retention of what we read in the New Testament or hear in conference, then we may want to:

1. Begin each study session with prayer. In humility and with faith invite the spirit of God, even the Holy Ghost, to assist in your learning.
2. Take time to ponder what you have read, with a prayer in your heart that the Spirit might attend you and inspire you in this process.
3. Write down any impressions you receive. Review and commit these to memory.
4. Follow the promptings of the Spirit, and do what you know to be right.
5. Avoid any influences that might distract from the Spirit.

I want to conclude this important chapter with this short story, told by Michael Allphin, my stake president. He said a mother in the stake had dropped off her two little boys for swimming lessons, more than a mile away from their home. The older boy was five. What the mother didn't know as she drove off was that the lessons had been cancelled that day. When she returned thirty minutes later, her boys were gone. After a frantic search of the area and adjacent streets, she decided to go home to recruit some help. There she found her two little boys. She asked the oldest how they had found their way home. He replied, "I knew part of the way. So I went as far as I knew, and the Holy Ghost led us the rest of the way."

May we have the faith and trust of a child to invite and allow the Spirit to lead us as we treasure up the words of eternal life.

Notes

1. Spencer W. Kimball, *The Teachings of Spencer W. Kimball*, 23.
2. James E. Talmage, Articles of Faith. Cited in *We Believe,* 416.
3. David A. Bednar, "That We May Always Have His Spirit to Be with Us," *Ensign*, May 2006, 28.
4. Ibid, 30.
5. Joseph Smith History in The Pearl of Great Price, 12.
6. Brigham Young, in the Bowery, Aug 17, 1856; Journal of Discourses 4:22; cited in *We Believe,* 416.
7. Henry B. Eyring, "As a Child," *Ensign*, May 2006.
8. David A. Bednar, ibid., 30.
9. Eldon Watson, *The Manuscript History of Brigham Young 1846–1847, 529* (23 Feb. 1847 entry). Quoted in Robert L. Millet, *Alive in Christ: The Miracle of Spiritual Rebirth*, 200–201.
10. *Teachings of Presidents of The Church* (Salt Lake City: The Church of Jesus Christ of Latter-day Saints), 46.
11. Millet, ibid., 200.
12. Orson Pratt, *Journal of Discourses*, XVII, 327.
13. Joseph Fielding Smith, Conference Report 1958; Oct 21. Cited in *We Believe,* 401.
14. Joseph Fielding Smith, *Take Heed to Yourselves*, 364. Cited in *We Believe,* 403.
15. David A. Bednar, ibid., 30.
16. Henry B. Eyring, ibid., 17.
17. David A. Bednar, ibid., 31.

3

THE ANATOMY OF A GREAT MEMORY

I imagine you will want to dive into discovering new and better ways to enhance your memory. However, before we jump into the Seven Habits of Highly Effective Learners and the associated strategies and techniques for memory enhancement, it seems prudent to take just a few pages to review what a good memory is composed of, and why it sometimes fails us.

Basically there are two different aspects to memory. The first I will call *natural memory*. This organic part of memory can be thought of as the soil or physiology of our mind. It includes the gray matter, the neurons, neurotransmitters, and other structures that make up the brain and its intricate communication systems. The second aspect of memory is sometimes referred to as *memory processes*. These are the developed or trained aspects of our memory—the procedures, strategies, and techniques that we employ, consciously or automatically, to remember things better or get the most out of our natural memory. In this book we will focus primarily on improving our memory processes. However, it's essential to have some understanding of both because they are inextricably tied together. In chapter 11 we will discuss ways that you can also optimize your soil—natural memory.

If our natural memory is not working well, the suggested strategies for memory enhancement won't work well either. This would be like having a new eight cylinder (V-8) vehicle with power steering and four wheel drive that can barely make it out of the garage because only four of the cylinders are firing. Conversely, even if our brain were running close to optimum naturally, if it is not organized, or if we are not employing strategies to make the most of its potential, we will continue to operate well below our capacity. We will get much farther faster and be able to accomplish much more with our memories if we can improve both aspects of memory.

The causes of most memory problems can be broken down into the following four interrelated categories: natural (physiology), processes, storage, and retrieval. These categories can be listed as follows:

Natural Storage	Storage Processes
Natural Retrieval	Retrieval Processes

Even though they have been placed into distinct categories, it's important to keep in mind that each of these memory functions interact with, and, to some extent, are dependent upon each other for optimal functioning or recall ability.

In order for our natural brain physiology to function properly for effective storage and retrieval, we need the following five things:

1. **Healthy cerebral cellular structures**—namely neurons, including axons, dendrites, and synapses. If these structures are not healthy, the necessary neurotransmitters will not be able to pass through to supply the messages needed for memory transmission.

2. **Neurotransmitters**—particularly acetylcholine, dopamine, and norepinephrine. These are the chemical messengers of the brain responsible for alertness as well as encoding, transferring, storing, and retrieving memories.

3. **Good nutrition**—to include a variety of proteins, vitamins, minerals, lipids or essential fatty acids (EFA), and carbohydrates. These are the building blocks and the fuel of the brain. They work together to create neurotransmitters and maintain cell membranes and other brain structures. Although it accounts for only two percent of our body weight, our brain burns twenty to thirty percent of the body's total available energy and requires a wide variety of nutrients.

4. **Plenty of oxygen**—The brain's various activities require a great deal of oxygen. We all know that when totally deprived of oxygen, brain cells can die within minutes. Less known is the fact that even a reduced consumption of oxygen, over time, can cause significant damage and memory problems.

5. **An effective circulatory system**—Since the brain cannot store the nutrients, calories, and oxygen it needs, it must constantly rely on a healthy, well-running delivery system. This may be thought of as the "Achilles' heel" of memory. Clogged arteries, or an otherwise sluggish circulatory system, can deprive the brain of the essential oxygen and other nutrients it needs to synthesize neurotransmitters and otherwise function properly. This is why exercise is so important for a healthy mind and memory.

For our memories to function at an optimal level, all the above noted elements need to be performing their own proper function and working in concert with each other, and not inhibited by any other harmful substances, including drugs or medications. If any one of these five elements is missing or seriously depleted, or if other substances are inhibiting proper brain function, it will usually manifest itself in some type of mental or memory deficit. Even a low-grade problem, in one or more of these areas over time, can result in memory storage or retrieval problems. In short, a person, thus afflicted, simply won't be able to recall what they want to, when they want to, even though they feel they ought to be able to.[1]

There are many reasons a person might experience problems with their natural memory physiology. The most common of these is vascular or circulatory problems. Therefore, it is always best to consult your physician or a neurologist if you are experiencing a significant decline in memory, to determine the most likely cause. (I did this once and it was very helpful.) Otherwise you could end up wasting a lot of time and money pursuing blind alleys when the light, in fact, lies at the end of another path. The nutrients (described in chapter 11) and strategies (described in chapters 4–10) in this book can prove useful in preventing or dealing with a wide variety of memory problems, but the more you know about your specific needs, the better you and your doctor will be able to develop a program that is effective for you.

Why We Can't Recall All We Read

The two basic processes of memory are *storage* and *retrieval.* Most of us feel that we have a problem with retrieval. We just can't remember what was read, said, or done. However, in reality the most common and correctable problems that prevent good recall are not in retrieval as much as in the way we store, or more correctly, do *not* store information. This is especially true as we grow older.

When most people talk of short-term memory, they are referring to the ability to remember events of the past day or hour. However, when neurologists or cognitive psychologists talk of short-term memory, they are referring to a much shorter time period. This is the time immediately after information is received, the period during which information either is or is not transferred into (recent) long-term memory. Short-term or temporary memory, as it is sometimes called, generally lasts only a few seconds, or at most a minute or two. For example, when someone tells you their phone number, "short-term" is the time between when you first hear the number and when you write it down or use it in making a call.

For example, if you were to look up a seven-digit phone number and then close the book, that number would stay in your head long enough for you to dial it, especially if you were to repeat it to yourself over and over. However, if someone were to interrupt this process and ask you for directions, in the short time it would take you to direct them, that 7-digit phone number would likely be lost from memory. Why? Because, unless you had, in that brief moment, activated some procedure for long-term storage, that number would not have been adequately recorded. This is the case for most of us. No doubt you have experienced this.

The same thing tends to happen when we are introduced to more than one person at a time or when we are reading. Our temporary memory usually does not retain information for an extended period, especially if it shifts focus to something else in the meantime. So if an interruption occurs before the number, name, or verse could be adequately stored in long-term memory, then for all practical purposes on earth,[2] it's gone for good. And you inevitably will have to go back to the source to retrieve it. You cannot draw it out of your memory, no matter how hard you try, if it was never adequately stored there in the first place.

As noted, inadequate storage—getting information from short-term or temporary memory into longer-term or more permanent memory—is the most common cause of memory problems, for young and old alike.

Above I described how interruptions or distractions can inhibit the adequate recording of memories. However, in reading the New Testament, you are likely to encounter a slightly different problem. This is technically referred to as "interference" or "displacement." As we read, new information tends to interfere with and displace previously read information in short-term memory. Therefore, if we want to be able to retain or later remember what we have read, it becomes imperative that we learn how to make those transfers from temporary to longer term memory as efficiently and impressive as possible, to avoid loss through fading, displacement, or other distractions. (How to do this will be explained in greater depth in other chapters. What follows here is a quick preview.)

Since we are constantly being interrupted, with new information coming in on top of previous inputs, you may be wondering, how do we manage to remember anything? Again the answer is, we actually don't remember most things we hear (especially if you are a man). We are able to recall more of what we see. And when we are able to recall what we have read, it's usually because we have somehow imagined or visualized what we were reading as we read about them. Most people can commit a picture to memory much faster and more indelibly than any written description of that picture.

This is pretty much an unconscious or automatic process. However, if we do not create those visual images with enough clarity and power to make a deep sensory impression, it's unlikely the information will be adequately stored in long-term memory. So it will, therefore, not be available for recollection or retrieval at any future point in time.

Fortunately sages and scholars down through the ages have developed various ways to consciously facilitate this process of transferring or storing information. By utilizing these methods, which I will elaborate on in the next seven chapters, you will be able to store wisdom and insights from the New Testament with such clarity and power that they will be available for retrieval and use days, weeks, months, even years later.

Here's an example of what I have been talking about and what we will be learning how to do later on in this book. Some years ago, while talking with a woman in a communication class I was teaching, I asked what her husband's name was. She told me, and I went on with the point I was trying to make. I then tried to refer back to her husband, but his name was not there. Somewhat embarrassed, I had to ask his name again. In an attempt to help me feel better, she noted, "Guess you didn't get it transferred from short- to long-term memory."

"You are right!" I said. "How do you know about that?"

"Well," she replied, "I was in your memory class last Spring."

"Yes, I thought you looked familiar," I replied. (Fortunately the class was large and only one session, which gave me a better excuse for not having remembered her in that setting.)

"Remember Lois Lane?" she asked.

"Yes, I do," I replied. Lois was the name of one of our class members. We used an association technique (described in chapter 6), pairing qualities of this Lois with Lois Lane, Superman's girlfriend, to burn her name into our brains. The point is we could both still remember that name and person after many months, with no rehearsal in between. However, since I had not applied any of these procedures to remembering her husband's name, it had slipped from my memory, even though she had told me only minutes before.

I think you should know that I am not an Einstein or a Harry Lorayne (a renowned memory expert). In fact, I believe I have a rather average natural memory, and I have had my share of problems remembering things, especially names. But fortunately I recognized this weakness early and so have sought long and hard to overcome it. At age seventeen, I read Harry Lorayne's *Instant Mind Power* and have been studying the topic of memory improvement ever since. I've attended various university courses on memory, both undergrad and postgraduate. I own several courses and more than twenty-five books on the subject. (See "Sources" at the end of this book for a listing of other excellent, up-to-date, books on this subject.) I have now taught the subject off and on for the past fifteen years, in various settings, including classes for senior citizens and their caretakers. I wouldn't call myself an expert, but I have learned a few things in the process of helping myself and others. What was once a weakness, has become a strength with the help of the Lord and serious study (see Ether 12:27). I hope this knowledge and experience can be of value to you and strengthen your memory.

But I want to warn you. Although the following methods can and do work amazingly well to improve memory and recall, as my embarrassing story illustrates, these principles and techniques will not work in helping you remember important information from the New Testament or conference *unless* you apply and practice them. You must learn and consistently apply, consciously or unconsciously, the following principles when you study and review the books of the New Testament or conference addresses, if you are to enjoy dramatically enhanced recall ability of that material. But if you do, I can promise you that you will.

Notes

1. There are a variety of prescription drugs that may negatively impact memory. If you suspect such an effect, discuss it with your doctor. Some of the nutrients noted in chapter 10 may help to counteract that adverse effect, but if you are on any type of prescription medication, it's wise to consult with your doctor before taking these.

2. There is evidence in the scriptures and near-death studies which suggests that when people are near death, some experience nearly total recall of past events in sensory rich detail. See *Lessons from the Light*, chapter 6, by Kenneth Ring (New York: Insight Books, 1998), for examples.

4

SEVEN HABITS FOR HIGHLY EFFECTIVE LEARNING

When asked how he governed his people, Joseph Smith stated, "I teach them correct principles and they govern themselves."[1] In order for each of us to effectively govern our mind and our memory, we must understand the principles related to memory. People who have outstanding recall abilities, either consciously or subconsciously, apply these principles and what I call the Seven Habits of Highly Effective Learners. These habits are built upon the foundation principles of effective memory—the principles that govern the storage and retrieval of information in the brain.

Most people understand what a habit is, but fewer understand the nature and value of principles. So let's review a few definitions. A principle is defined in the dictionary as (1) a fundamental truth or law as the basis of reasoning and action and (2) a law of nature or science.

This may remind you of Doctrine and Covenants 130:21: "And when we obtain any blessing from God, it is by obedience to that law upon which it is predicated."

Therefore, if we want to develop a good memory and be able to effectively recall insights and lessons from scripture, it would be wise to first gain a clear understanding of the laws or principles upon which a good memory or effective storage and retrieval is based. Then develop habits that are aligned with those principles.

In behavioral science, a principle is defined as "a statement about the relationship between two variables." (A variable is something that varies—increases or decreases, gets stronger or weaker—such as our ability to recall what we have read.) Typically this statement describes how a change in one of these variables (some action or behavior) affects another variable (result). In other words, how a change in A affects B. For example, one of the most basic principles of memory relates the act of rehearsal to recall ability and can be stated as follows: The more frequently and actively one rehearses information, the greater their ability to remember that information when needed. You can see from this that these statements of principle, like the dictionary suggests, reflect basic underlying laws of nature—in this case human nature, and more specifically, the nature of how our memory works, or how it is governed.

One of the nice things about principles and why I really enjoyed studying about them in graduate school is that once you understand the principles that govern behaviors or interactions in a given field, it's easier to determine appropriate specific behaviors in that area, and in this case appropriate habits to form. Moreover, underlying principles can be applied in many different settings and used to develop various methods or techniques that would be effective in novel situations or unchartered territory. For example, the rehearsal principle stated above can be applied to strengthening recall ability of information from almost any source in almost any area of study (science, religion, human relations, and so on).

Most of the basic principles for improving memory processes can be summed up with the acronym A RECORD. If you want to remember something, you just have to make A RECORD. Acronyms (using the first letter of the words you want to remember to form another word that will help remind you of each of the other words) are one of many methods[2] we will review to help facilitate recall.

However, before we get into this formula, I want to share something interesting about the word *record*. What I did not know when I developed that acronym and wrote my first book on remembering the Old Testament was that the word *record* has a deeper, older association with remembering. We tend to think of a *record* as being a written record, but in the beginning it was not so. In a recent FARMS article titled "What's in a Word? Etymology!" Cynthia L. Hallen notes:

> According to the Oxford English Dictionary, the verb *record* means 'to get by heart, to commit to memory, to go over in one's mind' (def. I1a). Etymologically speaking, to 're-cord' is to *learn things by heart so that we can ponder them again and again*. Records of personal and family history enable our children to 're-member' and 're-turn' to us. Scriptural records enable the hearts of the Lord's children to turn to the hearts of the prophets, and they enable righteous forebears to speak directly to the hearts of their descendants.[3]

I found that bit of insight very interesting in light of the following formula.

These then are the basic principles and habits of the A RECORD formula. The first **A** in this formula stands for *attention*. In order for Jesus' disciples to remember His words, they had to first pay attention. The same is true for us. Most of the time when we forget a verse of scripture or other bits of information, it is not a problem with our memory or retrieval system but that we just didn't pay close enough attention when the information was presented. Despite what you may have heard about recall under hypnosis, or subliminal learning, our brain simply does not effectively store everything that goes on around us or that passes through our fields of vision or within earshot. In order to remember something specific, we must first focus our attention and then get involved with that information. Highlighting or circling key words is one way to sharpen our attention. Generally we can only store well, for long-term retrieval, those things we have paid close attention to.

The Attention Principle: The more attention we pay to what we read or hear, the easier it will be to remember.

The Attention Habit: Pay close attention to, and get involved with, the material you wish to remember.

The following principles all reinforce attention and involvement.

The first **R** in RECORD stands for *relate*. Some experts feel this is the real key to effective storage and retrieval. As we read or hear new information, we find that it generally sticks best when we can relate or associate this in some memorable way with something else that we already know or have stored.

Jesus applied this principle often as He related his teachings to things the people were familiar with—sheep, wine, seeds. Thus He was able to help them to better remember His message.

This is one reason those who are older sometimes do better at retaining new information than those who are younger. They can *relate* better. They have more information and experiences to which they can tie or associate new information. This causes the new information to be more meaningful to them, which in turn causes them to pay better attention and leads them to becoming more involved in developing an image or related association that will clearly stick in long-term memory.

Most memory training methods, strategies, or techniques are simply ways people have developed to help them *relate* new information to more familiar knowledge. This is usually done with vivid memorable picture associations that relate the new with things they already know well. This in turn enables them to better recall the new things. In chapter 5 we will review a variety of these methods for relating or making vivid associations, to recall not only the teachings of the New Testament and general conference, but who taught them and where these teachings can be found.

The Relate Principle: The more we can relate new information to past easily recalled information, the easier it will be to remember the new information.

The Relate Habit: Relate new information in memorable ways (concrete, easily envisioned) with past familiar and easily recalled information.

The **E** in this formula stands for *envision.* Most people have better visual memories than auditory memories. For most of us, we are able to remember events, concepts, and ideas better if we can picture, visualize, or recreate them in our mind, rather than just reading or hearing about them. For example, most of us tend to remember pictures of a scene better than verbal descriptions of a scene. We tend to remember things we read better than things we hear, especially if a picture, diagram, chart, or other visual aid is included. You will note that most of the objects and symbols Jesus used in His illustrations like lilies, a gate, a candle, and a pearl were things that were easy for His audience to imagine or envision—and thus remember. The envision principle and the associated habit to be formed can be stated as follows:

The Envision Principle: The more vividly we can envision, or picture in our imagination, what we read or hear, the easier it will be to remember when needed.

The Envision Habit: Envision or picture what you wish to remember—with as much sensory rich detail and as vividly as you can.

The **C** stands for *concrete.* Concrete objects are much easier to visualize and thus remember than are abstract concepts or ideas. So again the metaphors Jesus used often contained concrete objects like salt, a beam, a house, and a vineyard to represent more abstract concepts or ideas. You may want to use additional objects to represent and remember other concepts discussed in the scriptures. For example, honor is a concept or idea that is not easily visualized. Therefore, to represent honor, you may want to visualize a sword or shield as to say, "I'm willing to fight for your honor." For love, you may use a heart; for honesty, a Boy Scout; for justice, a scale.

Because concrete symbols are easier to record and remember than concepts, we use graphic letters and words to represent ideas, and computer systems use icons or pictures to represent programs. This makes it easier to identify the program and recall the needed information. Most of us have pretty good natural memories. Like computers, we just need a concrete clue, hint, or symbol to remind us and enable us to access and pull up the fuller memory. The associated principle and habit here are:

The Concrete Principle: Concrete visible objects are pictured and remembered more easily than less tangible concepts or ideas.

The Concrete Habit: Picture more concrete objects or symbols to represent less tangible concepts or ideas.

The **O** stands for *organize* or put in order. In the Doctrine and Covenants, we are told to "organize [our]selves" (109:4). If you want a good memory, you need to follow that counsel. Good memories are organized memories. Paul said that "God is not the author of confusion" (1 Corinthians 14:33). Nor should we be in the things we want to commit to memory.

Like any file or retrieval system, if you want to be able to find what you want when you want it, you will need to enter it in an organized manner in the first place. Order makes access and retrieval much easier. Of course the New Testament is organized in a variety of ways—by author, sequentially, by date or time, spatially, by location, and numerically by chapter and verse. (In chapter 7 you will find another way to organize what you read and hear for easy recall.)

The reason I am able to communicate with you in writing is that we both share the same orderly, concrete writing system. This, as with all other writing systems, essentially organizes marks, which would otherwise be meaningless, into a mutually accepted and orderly system of symbols. It is because we both give the same orderly meaning to the same symbols and sounds that we are able to communicate and understand each other. Without this organization, there would be confusion and chaos. The biblical name for it was Babel for the babble that ensued.

A friend of mine, who you will read about in chapter 8, memorized the Sermon on the Mount, and in the process he discovered an order to these teachings that he had never seen before. Once he could see and understand this order, it made memorizing the sequence much easier.

The important thing here, however, is not so much how Jesus and His disciples organized their message, although that may help you, but that you organize it in your mind in a way that is meaningful to you. When you do, you will find it easier to remember and retrieve. The organize principle can be stated as follows:

The Organize Principle: The more we organize information in ways that are meaningful to us, the easier it will be for us to remember.

The Organize Habit: Organize what you wish to remember in ways that are meaningful to and memorable for you.

The second **R** stands for repeat, review, or *rehearse*. Repetition is considered the mother of memory. Perhaps that is why the Hebrews, particularly David and Solomon, used it so often in their writings, and why we have four accounts of the life and teachings of Christ. However, I prefer to use the verb *rehearse* in this formula, because it suggests a more involved, active (dynamic) process. Review or rehearsal sessions ideally should be set up within a few minutes after learning a new piece of information, then again within the hour, after a few hours, then the next day and again a few days later, then again a week later, and at regular intervals as needed thereafter. Spaced rehearsal is the key to long-term storage and recall. The Lord uses this principle in His Church. We are to attend meetings regularly, partake of the sacrament often, and study over and over the same gospel principles. In doing so, these teachings become more deeply ingrained in our brains and behaviors so that we remember to apply these in our daily lives when needed.

There is a principle in educational and behavioral psychology called over learning. The studies related to this suggest that the more we "over learn" a process or information, the easier it will be to access and apply. Perhaps that is what the Lord is trying to do with us through the various church programs. He wants us to learn the gospel so well that application becomes automatic. You will remember this rehearsal principle has already been stated as follows:

The Rehearsal Principle: The more frequently and actively we rehearses information, the greater our ability to remember that information when needed.

The Rehearsal Habit: Actively rehearse what you have learned at regular intervals as needed.

One way to rehearse and so better remember any new information is to fold a regular piece of notebook paper down the middle. On the outside fold, write questions on the material you want to recall. On the inside of that page, write the answers. Then during review sessions, just look at the questions and see if you can recall the answers. If you have difficulty recalling any of the answers, you may want to review the above noted principles for insights into what you could do differently. Then, using A RECORD as a guide, plus the following ideas in chapter 5, develop a strategy to impress that information more vividly into your memory. It's also helpful to make a note of your memory clues or cues on the opposite side of the inner fold.

The **D** is for *deliver*. We could call this the deliver paradox. After you receive and record new information, if you really want to retain it, you've got to give it away: deliver a lesson or sermon on it, or otherwise share[4] this information with others. And when there are no others around to share it with, you can deliver it out loud to yourself, as if you were delivering it to others. People you could share with might include your children, your neighbors' children, your spouse, your friends, fellow class members, whoever. Delivering what you have received to others deepens that knowledge. It's like a testimony that way. The more you share it, the stronger, and more firmly implanted, it becomes. No doubt the teachings of Jesus were reinforced in the minds of his apostles when they followed his command to teach what they had learned to the world (see Matthew 28). This process likely helped them to retain his words until they were written down in the gospels. Accordingly, the more we deliver or share with others what we learn from the New Testament and conference, the more deeply these will become imbedded into our own memories.

The Lord gives an interesting promise in Doctrine and Covenants 88:78: "Teach ye diligently and my grace shall attend you, that you may be instructed more perfectly in theory, in principle, in doctrine, in the law of the gospel, in all things that pertain unto the kingdom of God, that are expedient for you to understand."

Note the Lord says that when we teach diligently, by the grace of God, we are "instructed more perfectly." Teaching apparently facilitates the teacher's learning.

Most teachers will tell you that they learn much more in preparing and delivering their lessons than their students do. Why? First, because they have to pay closer attention, get more involved, relate it to other information, think of ways to make it clearer, and so on. Second, because in the process of delivery, the information is burned more deeply into their own memories. I remember learning this principle as a child in Primary when I had to give a two-and-a-half-minute talk. I found I learned a lot more from that experience than when I just sat and heard other kids give their talks. It's a true principle that can be stated as follows:

The Deliver Principle: The more we deliver or share what we have learned, the greater our ability will be to remember that information when needed.

The Deliver Habit: Deliver or share new information that you have learned with others, or at least deliver it to yourself, in a dramatic or memorable way.

The Seven Principles for Making a Memorable RECORD

In review, the A RECORD formula and principles are as follows:

A is for *attention*: The more attention we pay to whatever we see or hear, the easier it will be to remember.

R is for *relate*: The more we can relate new information to past easily recalled information, the easier it will be to remember the new information.

E is for *envision*: The more vividly we can envision, or picture in our imagination, what we read or hear, the easier it will be to remember when needed.

C is for *concrete*: Concrete visible objects are pictured and remembered more easily than less tangible concepts or ideas.

O is for *organize*: The more we organize information in ways that are meaningful to us, the easier it will be for us to remember.

R is for *rehearse*: The more frequently and actively we rehearse information, the greater our ability to remember that information when needed.

D is for *deliver*: The more we deliver or share what we have learned, the greater our ability to remember that information when needed.

How to Remember the A RECORD Formula

It will be important for you to cement this formula into your brain, because these seven principles provide the foundation you will need for the procedures and techniques that follow. Moreover, if you experience some type of difficulty in recalling information from your studies, these can provide a good checklist for troubleshooting. Finally with an awareness of these principles, you will be able to add your own memory techniques as needed.

Since an awareness of each point in this formula is so essential to understanding all that follows, I want you to take a few minutes right now to commit it to memory. Make sure this acronym and its related principles are firmly fixed in your long-term memory before you go on. To do this, I want you to apply some of the principles and methods we have just learned.

If you've read to this point, at least you've been giving this formula a significant amount of *attention*. Plus you have *related* the acronym A RECORD with its associated principles. If you have also *envisioned* or pictured yourself doing these things as we went along, that should have helped to etch them into your brain, especially if your images were *concrete* enough. You see that by relating these principles to the acronym you have an *organized* way to remember them. Plus you will note that they are organized pretty much sequentially (whenever you go about remembering something, you will typically go through this process in this order). In fact, that is the major habit or sequence for learning that we need to *rehearse*, over and again. And then *deliver* to or share with someone else. By now you should have it stored up there fairly well. But just to make sure, here is little exercise that I would now like you to try.

I would like you to put down this book, and on the left hand side of a blank sheet of paper, write this acronym vertically as follows:

A
R
E
C
O
R
D

If you can't remember all seven letters, just think: "In order for me to remember what I read in the New Testament or hear in conference, I must be like the prophets of old, and make A RECORD of those things that I wish to remember.

Once you have the letters A RECORD written vertically on your paper as shown above (but without looking at the book), go back and from memory write down what each letter stands for. If you miss a principle, look it up, but then put the book down and fill it in from memory.

Now, turn the paper over, and think of the acronym clue phrase: "In order for me to remember, I must be like the prophets of old, and make A RECORD." Then write down the letters vertically, as noted above. Next, note to the right what each stands for and as much of its associated principle as you can recall. As you do this, envision or see yourself doing each step with some information you are learning or would like to remember from the New Testament. When you are done with this, you should have this acronym and these seven principles of memory pretty well chiseled into your brain. But just to make sure the image doesn't fade, I want you to do this little exercise once more after you are done with this chapter, and then again tomorrow, the next day, and at least once next week and each week thereafter for the next month. By then, if you've been using this formula, the acronym will be well set in your mind and ready to apply anytime, and anywhere.

One Additional Important Principle

Above I noted that "most" of the basic principles for improving memory processes can be summed up with the acronym A RECORD. One important additional principle we need to review is the meaningful principle. This can be stated as follows:

The Meaningful Principle: The more meaningful something is for us, the more likely we are to remember it.

The Meaningful Habit: When in doubt, clarify the meaning behind the words you read or hear.

Jesus noted there were some who saw what He did and heard what He said, but nevertheless, they did not understand His words (see Matthew 13:13; Luke 8:10). In other words, although they heard what He was saying, they could not understand what He meant. And if they could not understand the meaning in His words, they would likely not remember it. As noted in chapter 2, understanding and remembering are both gifts from the same spirit, but it's hard to remember if one doesn't first understand.

Like the other principles in this chapter, this too has broad application. In fact, this idea is a given, mentioned or implied in each of the other A RECORD principles. Nevertheless, because of its pivotal importance, it is worthy of special mention, and it will be helpful to have in mind as we discuss four additional ideas for improving reading comprehension. First, however, I'd like to explain how this relates to and why it's a "given" for the other principles.

Initially we are likely to pay more *attention* to things that have a special meaning for us, especially if we can *relate* them to something else that is meaningful. It is usually easier to *envision* things that are meaningful, especially if they are *concrete*. And the meaning we give to these concrete, easily envisioned items or icons is important in developing a memorable picture that reminds us of the text. For example, once a missionary understands that the seeds mentioned in Jesus' parable of the sower represent the word of God, and he understands the meaning of the other symbols in this story, this parable will have much more significance and relevance for them, and thus be easier to remember.

Additionally, one of the objectives in *organizing* information is to make it more meaningful for us, and as that principle notes, "the more we organize information in ways that are *meaningful* to us, the easier it will be for us to remember." *Rehearsal* is much more effective if we are rehearsing information that is meaningful to us, as opposed to nonsense. And finally, it is easier to *deliver* or share information if it's meaningful. In fact, our brains are wired such that if something does not have meaning, our brain will impose meaning as we talk about it. This is the idea behind the famous Rorschach psychological assessment in which the person is asked to describe what he sees in an inkblot. My wife can do the same thing with clouds. That's how the brain works. It has a strong natural tendency to impose meaning on things that are ambiguous or unclear, perhaps because "meaning" really is an essential part of understanding and memory.

However, there are times when we are reading that we "just don't get it." We don't understand the meaning the author is trying to convey. This is especially true for children when they are reading or listening to scripture. It can be a real problem, even for adults, in comprehending and remembering the New Testament. If you don't get it, if you don't understand what the author is talking about, you are not going to be able to envision it or remember it. Or worse, your recollections will be erroneous. Therefore, one of the main obstacles to understanding is vocabulary. If you don't know the meaning of some of the words, or figures of speech you encounter, then you likely won't capture or retain the message. Because the King James Bible was translated from an ancient foreign language into an archaic form of English, much of it is hard for the average American to comprehend. How can we gain a better understanding of the intended meaning of a text so that we can more accurately and effectively remember it? There are basically four methods. They are pretty much common sense but worth repeating. Whenever you are reading and find that you are not understanding what you have just read, do the following four things:

1. Go back to where you did understand and proceed from there, until you run into a word or two that you don't understand.

2. Look up any new words or words that are hard to understand in the Bible dictionary in the back of your LDS Bible. It doesn't have every odd word, but it has many of them. Additionally, you may be able to use the topical guide to see other contexts in which the word has been used. You can also use the footnotes, which often provide other wording of the text or references to related scriptures. Another text that I like is *The New Testament for Latter-day Saint Families—with Helps for Children* (that brings it down to my level) published by Deseret Book. In this book and related editions of the standard works, nearly all the important difficult words and verses are explained in extensive footnotes. Of course there are also many commentaries, most of which are available in LDS electronic libraries for easy access. "If in doubt, check it out." Look up the meaning of the words being used.

3. If you are just tired or distracted, stop. Put the book down. Get up and go get a drink of water, climb some stairs, or take a bit of a walk to wake yourself up. If you are distracted by something important, find a piece of paper and write down what it is that you are thinking about. Once your distracting thoughts are down on paper, your brain will feel more comfortable letting you go back to your reading.

4. Employ other active learning strategies from this book, like imagining the interaction from the scenes you are reading about, or summarizing and then drawing a diagram of the chapter, and/or significant symbols (pictures) from the text. See chapter 6 for additional mental activities to help you remember who said what and where. All of these strategies will help you to stay focused and remember.

If you are actively applying the seven habits, it's less likely you will need to use these steps. So let's just review those habits one more time.

The Seven Habits of Effective Learners in Review

The Attention Habit: Pay close attention to, and get involved with, those things that you wish to remember.

The Relate Habit: Relate new information in memorable ways (concrete, easily envisioned) with past familiar and easily recalled information.

The Envision Habit: Envision or picture what you wish to remember—with as much sensory rich detail and as vividly as you can.

The Concrete Habit: Picture more concrete objects or symbols to represent less tangible concepts or ideas.

The Organizing Habit: Organize what you wish to remember in ways that are meaningful to and memorable for you.

The Rehearsal Habit: Actively rehearse what you have learned at regular intervals as needed.

The Deliver Habit: Deliver or share new information that you have learned with others, or at least deliver it to yourself, in a dramatic or memorable way.

Now we can move on to some amazingly effective ways to apply and optimize these principles and habits.

Notes

1. Joseph Smith, *Millennial Star*, (15 November 1851), 339.
2. These are often referred to as "mnemonic" devices. The term mnemonic (pronounced "newmonic") is derived from Mnemosyne, the Greek goddess of memory. The early Greeks invented some of these methods.
3. Cynthis L. Hallen. Online. *What's in a Word? Etymology!* Provo, Utah: FARMS, 2003, 105–107. Available from farms.byu.edu/display.php?table=jbms&id=306.
4. We could call this the "share" principle, but "S" does not fit our acronym. Plus sharing implies a need for others, while you can "deliver" a sermon to yourself with similar effect. But in your mind you should associate "deliver" with sharing, or teaching the information to others.

5

THE AMAZING MEMORY METHODS—TEN OPTIMIZING STRATEGIES

The crowd was amazed when Toby Roebuck, a young sixteen-year-old boy from Ohio, was able to recite the contents of virtually any page in the most recent edition of a major metro magazine. How on earth could he do that? He was not a genius or a savant. He did not have a photographic memory. So I was very curious to find out what his method was. When I met Toby, he was much older, now a successful mortgage broker in Alameda, California. He had attended one of my classes at the local stake center. After class, we had a chat, and he shared with me the basics of how he did it.

A few weeks later in Mesa, Arizona, I met Dr. Lane Bigler, who had learned and applied similar techniques to get through med school and then helped other medical students to remember their coursework. He noted that those who had learned and applied his techniques consistently scored at the top of their classes. His example is a second witness to the efficacy of these methods.

In Logan, Utah, I was told of another man who, years ago, had learned a way to remember the location of scriptures. At family reunions he would invite family members to try and stump him by asking the location of any Bible story or notable verse. But no one could. He always knew the stories' locations and content. Fortunately, these are not isolated cases. As I've traveled around teaching and talking about methods for improving memory, I've met many people who have learned and used similar strategies to accomplish phenomenal feats with their memory.

Toby was gracious enough to send me a faded copy of his old training manual. What I found was a set of memory techniques commonly referred to by psychologists as mnemonics.[1] Memory experts have been aware of most of these for many years. As I noted in chapter 3, I first read of them in Harry Lorayne's book in 1967. I know Kenneth Higbee, Ph.D., has been teaching them at BYU and at BYU Education Weeks for at least the last thirty years, and Dr. Truman Madsen taught them there before Higbee. However, the average person hardly knows they exist, even though most of us have used some type of mnemonic, or memory aid, at one time or another.

In the next three chapters we will review the most relevant of these techniques and how we can apply them to learning and remembering scripture. You will note that most of these strategies are based on one or more of the principles in the A RECORD formula—particularly the envision and relate or associate principles—and are in fact simply ways to make these mental pictures and associations more powerful and memorable.

Avoiding the Profane

There is a problem with some memory methods, however—at least for me. Most of the books on memory enhancement strategies suggest that for an association to be vivid or most memorable, it needs to be in some way bizarre, exaggerated, distorted, indecent, farcical, zany, ludicrous, or outrageous—anything but ordinary.

While bizarre and zany techniques may be okay when trying to recall jokes or pop magazine articles, they seem inappropriate for remembering the doctrines of salvation or the teachings of Christ. On the other hand, the idea that "unusual" or "extraordinary" things are more easily remembered is undeniable. Likely one reason Joseph Smith was able to accurately recount what the angel Moroni taught him in his room, as recorded in the Pearl of Great Price, was that this visitation was so extraordinary, as well as the fact that it was "rehearsed" three times. Who does not recall the story of Jesus walking on the water or Lazarus coming forth from the grave? Each of these stories is made more memorable by the fact that they evoke some very unusual images.

What's Your Learning Style?

Before we get into the optimizing strategies, I want to touch on one other important concept—learning style. Most people, for example, better remember the things that they see, but some retain better what they hear. Whichever modality you prefer will make a difference in determining which of the following strategies will work best for you. Most of these were developed for those with a visual preference. Numbers 9 and 10, however, are usually most effective for those with an auditory preference.

Additionally, some people are able to study and concentrate better in the morning, and others do better in the evening. Most learn better on their own in peace and quiet, but some seem to learn better interacting with others or with music in the background. Some study best sitting in a firm chair at a table where they can take notes as they go; others might do better sitting in a bean bag. It's helpful if each of us can take some notes as to when and where we learn best, in order that we might create the optimal environment for learning.

Appendix A contains a short survey you may want to take to help determine your preferred learning style and modality.

Ten Methods for Creating Indelible Images

As noted in the envision principle in the previous chapter, we are able to remember stories and ideas much better if we can create a clear, vivid picture of them in our minds. Here then are ten effective ways to make those mental images and associations more vivid and memorable:

1. Anchor what you read to a specific location real or imaginary.

Most memories are lost because they are not tied down. They are not anchored to or associated with anything in particular. So, like a reed raft that is not tied to its harbor, these memories are soon swept out to the sea of lost memory, never to be seen or recalled again, unless by accident. How is this to be prevented? Simply by anchoring these memories to something familiar, filing or picturing them in a place that we can easily recall and go back to in our minds where we can always find them.

This strategy is at least as old as the ancient Greeks and was probably used before them. The Greeks referred to it as the loci system—*loci* being the root for the word *location*. We know that when Greek orators were preparing their speeches, they would imagine walking through the various rooms of their house or some other familiar building and visualize each of their main ideas or points in a different room or location. When they later delivered their speeches, they would again imagine themselves being in this location strolling through the various rooms, in the sequence they had planned, seeing and relating the associated points made in each room as they went along.

If you have a good "loci" memory, or memory for locations, you will be able to locate information much more easily by following a similar procedure for storage and retrieval. This strategy can be used to remember any sermon or story. All you have to do is come up with a location that you are familiar with, where you can envision or anchor the elements of the sermon, story, or chapter that you want to remember.

In applying this strategy, you can either use a location where you have lived or spent time, such as your own yard, your neighborhood, a city park, or some mental replication of the location being talked about. But since we have no photos of how biblical locations originally looked (they may appear similar now, but they were not the same 2000 years ago), this would need to be a place you re-create in your own imagination.

For example, if you wanted to remember the Sermon on the Mount, you could envision this taking place on a hill you are familiar with or at a local park. Or you could imagine the mountain (likely more of a hill or knoll) back near Galilee where Jesus taught. You may want to use an artist's rendition to help you create a mental image of the location. But wherever you envision this, what is important is that you create a clear mental image of this location and imagine the events or teachings occurring in this setting. Then imagine that same setting each time you think of this event. That way you will always know where to go in your mind to find that particular bit of information.

2. Put yourself in the picture.

We will likely feel more involved and remember better if we can imagine being there. Have you ever been on a ride in Disneyland or another theme park where a 360° picture is displayed all around you, so you feel as if you were right there? If you experienced this, you likely have not forgotten it. With a little practice, you can do the same thing in your mind with scripture stories. In fact, we do this all the time when we dream. We don't just watch the action, we are involved in it.

With the Sermon on the Mount, I imagine myself in the front row of the crowd not more than five yards from where Jesus is standing when he begins his sermon with "Blessed are the poor in spirit for theirs is the kingdom of heaven." I then imagine myself farther back, above the crowd, at about eye level, where I can imagine the various elements of his message being acted out or displayed in this setting. See examples below and in chapter 8.

3. See the action and interaction in the story or text.

See things rising, falling, twisting, jerking, expanding, shrinking, and so forth. Also imagine the interactions between the various people. The Bible uses a lot of great imagery and action verbs to assist here. For example, it's easy to imagine Jesus' disciples in their fishing boat being tossed in the storm, or the pressing throngs of people reaching out to grab the hem of Jesus garment, or Stephen being stoned. Therefore, we can all remember these stories. But it may also be helpful to utilize action imagery to envision more conceptual teachings like "blessed are the peacemakers" (Matthew 5:9). For this you might imagine two people shaking hands and exchanging olive branches or white handkerchiefs, and then Jesus blessing them. Another of Jesus' teachings that would be conducive to action imagery would be His parable about the wise man who built his house upon a rock, and then came the rain, floods, and wind (see Matthew 7:24–25). Creating this sort of action imagery can be fun, and most of the elements for doing so are already in the text, or otherwise easily created. Such a picture vividly imagined will not soon be forgotten.

4. Create unusual or extraordinary images or associations.

As we noted above, images that are extraordinary are more easily remembered. If you saw a dog bite a man, it may get your attention, but it's not that extraordinary. However, if you saw a man bite a dog, that would likely be more memorable. One common technique in this category is to amplify your images. You may want to imagine some things larger, taller, bigger, fatter, or in some other way more exaggerated than normal. When Jesus talks about removing the "beam" from our own eye, do we imagine a microscopic sliver, or something much larger? Likely a larger piece of wood, would make that scene harder to forget. You can also alter or amplify the shape or color of images in your picture. (You will see how I use this below to help distinguish text from memory cues.)

I do not add many unusual elements to the New Testament stories themselves, since most are extraordinary enough. This technique is most useful when used to remember the location of important scriptures. See the number peg system in chapter 6 for additional illustrations of this method.

5. Visualize what you are reading in sensory rich detail, including color, sounds, touch, and maybe even taste or smells.

Do your New Testament images have color? Can you imagine the sounds or smells associated with the events you are reading about? Or are yours all silent pictures? Generally the more sensory-rich details we can add to our images, the more vivid and memorable they will be.

Some people naturally experience these senses more than others, and recalling a certain feel, taste, or smell can evoke associated memories. But even if you are sensory challenged to some degree, by adding or imagining these other senses in play in your mental pictures, you can help bring the New Testament stories more to life and make your images more memorable. So as you imagine Jesus' celebrated entry into Jerusalem, you might imagine the green palm branches covering His path, the various colored clothing of the different classes of people, the feel and smell of the donkey, the cheers of the crowds, and so on.

6. Feel the feelings or emotion in the scene or story.

Can you empathize with the characters? Can you imagine how the key people involved must have felt? How did the rich young ruler feel when Jesus told him to go and sell all that he had and come and follow Him? How about the prodigal son, or the father of the prodigal son? What feelings did they experience? Going back to Jesus' triumphal entry, can you imagine the excitement in the air as Jesus rode into Jerusalem in fulfillment of prophecy? Can you imagine Jesus' righteous indignation as He drove the money changers from the temple, or as He denounced the hypocrisy among the Pharisees who were constantly trying to trick Him? Can you imagine the profound shock Paul must have felt on the road to Damascus when he saw a light and heard a voice informing him that he was fighting against God (kicking against the pricks) and needed to change his ways? Often when we can't remember the words, we can still recall the feelings. By putting ourselves in the place of these characters or at least trying to empathize with them, we can deepen our appreciation for what they went through and improve our recall of the message.

7. Mentally rotate the image or see the scene from a different perspective.

There is usually more than one way to view or re-create an image or scene. If you find your first image less than memorable, try imagining the scene from a different angle or perspective. How would the Sermon on the Mount look from the bottom of the hill, or from Jesus' perspective? How about when Jesus raised the boy with palsy who had been lowered through the roof? What would that scene have looked like from the roof? Can you imagine the scene with the woman at the well from the woman's perspective? Sometimes visualizing a scene from a different angle or perspective can make it more memorable.

8. Draw pictures and symbols to represent key concepts.

Most people better remember things they write down. Moreover, as we noted in conjunction with the envision principle in the last chapter, we tend to remember pictures we've drawn better than words we've written. Symbols are easily pictured objects used to represent common concepts. Jesus used symbols common to his culture all the time in his teachings—a yoke, a gate, water, wine. So can we.

You don't need to use symbols created by others. In fact, it will be better if you can create your own. Just note whatever comes to mind. For example, in order to remember "the fruit of the Spirit" as described by Paul in Galatians 5, you could imagine a chocolate heart or two people hugging to represent love, a person jumping up and down to represent joy, a dove or a man sitting holding an olive branch to represent peace. As with other methods mentioned here, creating your own symbols to represent concepts can be a lot of fun. Children can even get involved in this as a travel game while riding in the car.

In Galatians 5, Paul notes seven fruit of the Spirit. I have provided symbols for the first three. How would you symbolize the last four?

When we draw these symbols, we are creating both a kinesthetic or sensory memory as well as a visual impression. Of course, the more involved you become in developing these, the more attention you will pay to text, and the more you will remember. You don't have to be an artist like Arnold Friberg either. Stick figures work just fine. Pen or pencil doodles are great, just so long as you know what they stand for. These are not only especially helpful for us visual learners, but also for those who are more right brained, those with greater tactile sensitivity, and any other creative individuals. (See Mapping Your Memories, chapter 7, for a well-developed system that makes good use of this technique.)

9. Read aloud and discuss.

When we read aloud with emphasis and expression, we add new auditory pathways to our memory. This is true for predominantly visual learners as well as those with an auditory preference, although it's of greatest value to the latter.

It would likely also be helpful for all of us to discuss our reading on a regular basis with a partner and include in that discussion how we might apply these teachings to our own lives. (That's why we have Sunday School classes, where teachers are counseled in the manual to involve class members, "that all may be edified of all" [D&C 88:122]).

10. Record and listen. One extension of the previous method is recording the text or a selected portion (see chapter 9 for illustrations) onto a cassette tape and then playing it to yourself at intervals when your hands and eyes are occupied with other things but your ears are not—as when driving in your car. Times like these also provide another good opportunity to envision the lessons being heard and to try other optimizing strategies.

Some research suggests our own voice may be more memorable than someone else's. In fact, if you have a lyrical mind, or like to sing, you may want to put the words you are trying to remember to song and then record the song and sing along with it.

One of the most important keys here is that whenever we employ one of these image or memory enhancement techniques, we have to first pay close attention and become involved with the text and message. As a result, it can't help but become more memorable for us. (You can see how others get involved with the text and employ these techniques in chapters 7, 8, and 9.)

Linking Concepts for Recall and Application

The ten strategies noted above are powerful, and can indeed help to optimize our mental images and thus greatly improve the quality of memory storage and the ease of retrieval. However, this is only true if we use them. If after reading these you say, "Oh, yes, that makes sense. I could do that," but then you don't, what good will these do you? The answer is, practically no good at all. I now want to show you a way to remember these for future application.

In chapter 9 I will show you a method for making the application of these techniques a habit, and in chapter 6 you will learn a technique for recalling these by their number. But first, because they are so important, I want to share with you one other method for burning these ten optimizing strategies into your brain for future reference. Moreover, this technique can be used to "link," or string together and remember any list of items, concepts, or ideas, including the order of the books of the New Testament or speakers at general conference. Thus it is called the link method.

This method is an extension of the interaction technique noted above, and employs both the relate and envision principles. Yet it is really quite simple to learn. In fact, for that reason, it is often the first technique taught in memory training courses. All you have to do is this:

Envision a memorable interaction between items or key elements in your list.

Of course, in order to make these interactions more memorable, it will be helpful to apply some of the other ten techniques as you go. I will get you started by providing the key elements of each strategy and the interconnections I have envisioned for the first five, so you can see how this works. All you have to do is come up with images to link the last five.

1. **Anchor what we read** to a specific location real or imaginary.
2. **Put yourself in the picture**.

3. **See the actions and interaction** among the elements in your picture.
4. **Create unusual or extraordinary** images or associations.
5. **Visualize what you are reading in sensory-rich detail.**

To help me remember these five techniques, I imagine myself stepping into my backyard where I see a huge anchor from a ship, a giant plasma TV screen, and a waist-deep stream with John the Baptist baptizing people. "This is extraordinary," I say to myself. My backyard and anchor remind me to anchor my memories to a familiar place. I imagine myself stepping through the TV screen—putting myself into the picture. There I not only see John the Baptist in his camel hair attire, but I can hear him calling out, "Repent ye, for the kingdom of heaven is at hand" (Matthew 3:2). As I bend down, I can feel the water running through my fingers. Standing next to the water is a film director who calls, "Action!" I then watch as John baptizes several people. So, there you go! With that simple scene in mind, it should be easy to remember these five techniques. However, when you do this, you will want to remember your own backyard or some other place you are very familiar with.

Now it's your turn. Here are the last five strategies. Just think of some concrete way to represent each as you go and then link them together in some zany or unusual scene. As you do so, apply some of these techniques to make your images vivid and memorable. You may choose to continue my picture or come up with one of your own. Have fun!

6. **Feel the feelings or emotion** in the scene or story.
7. **Mentally rotate the image** or see the scene from a different perspective.
8. **Draw pictures and symbols** to represent key concepts.
9. **Read aloud and discuss.**
10. **Record and listen.**

One of the added bonuses to using the link method is that the more we use our imagination to create vivid pictures and dynamic or unusual associations and interactions, the more creative we will become.

Remembering the Seven Fruit of the Spirit

Now let's put this method to practical use. Earlier I mentioned Paul's seven fruit of the Spirit. In light of the admonitions in chapter 2 to seek and be guided by the Holy Ghost, this list from Paul could be very useful in helping us to know when we have, or are being led by, the Spirit. To enable us to remember those seven qualities, it might be helpful if we used the link system as well as some of the ten optimizing strategies. This is how you might begin to accomplish that.

Since these are all abstract qualities, it will help if we have first created concrete symbols to represent each quality. I started to do this under number 8 above for love, joy, and peace. Hopefully you finished that. Next, all we need to do is link these symbols together in some memorable way. So if your symbol for *love* was a hug, you could start out by imagining two people hugging. To put myself in the scene, I would imagine that I am one of those two, and my wife the other. For an anchor I would imagine this occurring underneath the neighbor's apple (fruit) tree. Then, when I want to recall the seven fruit of the Spirit, all I have to do is remember this fruit tree and the associated scenes, and the seven qualities will be there.

After the hug (*love*), I would imagine jumping up and down for *joy*! As I do so, I bump into a lawn chair where my neighbor is sitting with an olive leaf in hand and a *peace*ful smile on his face. He's not even disturbed by my clumsy actions.

Now, can you imagine some interactions with the other symbols you created for longsuffering (patience), gentleness, goodness, and faith?

Remembering General Conference

As I was preparing this chapter, a friend told me about a visit by a General Authority to a remote mission in the Church, not long after a semi-annual general conference. Unfortunately, at least some of the missionaries had not been able to hear conference, so one Elder asked the question, "What did they talk about at conference?" Perhaps he intended a brief summary of the general theme, but their visiting Authority was able to go right down the list and note every speaker and what he spoke about. The Elders were amazed. But you can do that as well with the link method or some variation thereof.

I'm not sure what this brother's method was, but here's how I did that with the April 2006 Sunday morning session. First, I selected an anchor location, which for me was the North Visitor's Center on Temple Square. It could have been anywhere, but when I think of conference, Temple Square comes to mind. Plus, several of the speakers spoke of Christ, and there is a large statue of Christ in this building. And I was once a guide there, so I am familiar with its layout.

Second, if I was not familiar with a speaker, I came up with a way to help me remember his name. I will explain this method more in the next chapter but will illustrate it here.

Next, as each person spoke, I took notes (see chapter 7) and visualized his message using the above-noted principles and strategies, in sensory-rich detail. In the process, each speaker was integrally linked with his message.

Finally, I visualized each succeeding speaker linked or associated in some memorable way with the previous speaker. That way I can easily identify who the next speaker or the previous speaker was. I then see his message being portrayed in an adjacent setting, which again helps me to anchor that information in a concrete location that will be easy to recall to mind.

That may seem a bit complicated, but it is actually easier to do than to explain. This, then, is how that picture of Sunday's conference sessions all flows together for me. (In the interest of space, I will only give the gist of each person's talk.) The first speaker was Elder Faust. He spoke of the restoration. I see him giving this address at the top of the stairs as you come in the front entrance. There used to be a picture there of some of the leaders of the reformation and their statements regarding the need for a restoration. Elder Faust has a microphone in his hand, and I see him handing it to Elder Holland, who then proceeds through the corridor and up the ramp to the statue of Christ. As he walks along, he talks to those who are down or depressed (I see them with their heads down; they look depressed), and he leads them up to Christ, which is his central message—"Come unto Christ [for] He knows the way up."

I see Elder Holland end his address back down on the main floor at the bottom of the ramp near the last of the pictures depicting the life of Christ, where he hands the microphone to Elder Tingey. I'm not as familiar with Elder Tingey, so I imagine a co-worker whose last name is Tingey. He brings the group back up to the picture of Jesus praying in Gethsemane. On the way, he reminds the group of the nail prints in Jesus' hands on the statue and begins to talk about the Atonement and the great plan of happiness for God's children.

After Elder Tingey's address, he escorts the group into the little theater, where they are met by a woman with a small green pine tree in her hand. This is to remind me that her name is Sister Pingree. She places the tree down on the stage, and it rapidly begins growing up. She then goes on to talk about growing up in the service of the Lord. At the end of her address, I see Elder Oaks step onto the stage and take the microphone. He then selects different people from the audience with apparently diverse ethnic and cultural backgrounds and tells them how "the gospel is for everyone." As he concludes, he invites them to follow him back to the front foyer where we see and hear President Hinckley share from his journal and bear his testimony to conclude the morning session.

For the afternoon session, I see Elder Ballard on the south steps talking about missionary work. Elder Scott takes the mike from him and in the other hand holds up the *Preach My Gospel* manual which he extols as he continues talking about missionary work. When he is done, he tosses the mike across the lawn where it hits one of the stones on the wall of the tabernacle. A man picks it up. His name is Elder David Stone. He tells the people about creating a Zion here in the midst of Babylon.

The next speaker asks to have the mike placed on the end of a long wooden board. His name is Elder Wood. As soon as he begins speaking, a verbal fight breaks out in the crowd with some anti-Mormon demonstrators. He addresses both sides on the importance of avoiding slander and stereotyping. Then the next speaker takes the mike, and steps into a small patch of quicksand and gets stuck. He's Elder Stucki. Immediately I see him begin to pray. Three large stepping stones are thrown into the pit by family members, which he uses to step out of the muck. These represent prayer, faith, and family—three stepping stones to eternal happiness—the topics of his talk.

Next I see Elder Wirthlin take the mike and climb up onto an old white horse called Snowman. The horse walks around to the south side of the tabernacle where they both take a drink from the fountain. Elder Wirthlin then talks about drinking deeply of living water and the abundant life. He then gives the mike to President Hinkley, standing nearby, who admonishes us all to *remember* and live the counsel we have received.

So there in a nutshell are the April 2006 Sunday sessions of conference all linked together. As I said earlier, it's actually harder to explain than to do. Of course, it took more effort to visualize the content of each talk, but now all I have to do is recall to mind this scene at the North Visitor's center and voila, both Sunday sessions are right there for ready access, in sequence, out of sequence, by topic, or speaker. Now you try it.

See appendix B for an example of how this linking method can be used to remember the books of the New Testament in order.

For additional examples and tips on enhancing mental images and creating memorable links, check out our Web site at www.ARECORD4LDS.com.

6

HOW TO REMEMBER WHO SAID WHAT AND WHERE TO FIND IT

Let's say you home teach or visit teach a person who has been offended by another member and is having a hard time getting past that. Where can you find Jesus' counsel on dealing with offenses or forgiveness? You recall that Jesus taught on at least two occasions that if we cannot forgive others, our Heavenly Father may not forgive us. But where is that located? Where can we find the golden rule, His admonition against anger, or the signs He gave of events to precede His second coming? And just for fun, where did Jesus give the counsel that could be considered a warning against the practice of polygamy? Where did he say, "No man can serve two masters?"

What if you were talking with a Christian friend of another faith who didn't believe in the necessity of baptism, or apostles and prophets, or the laying on of hands for the gift of the Holy Ghost? Do you know where to find scriptures to support each of those doctrines in the New Testament? What if your friend could not accept the Joseph Smith story because he or she was taught the Father and Son were the same person, or that God did not have a body? Could you show your friend verses from the New Testament to support the First Vision?

Indeed the New Testament is full of great counsel, comforting doctrines, and divine insights into not only how to deal with the challenges of this life but the way to eternal life and happiness. The teachings of Jesus and the epistles of Paul and the other apostles contain timeless guidance and wisdom for members and nonmembers alike. But if we can't find it when we need it, if we can't remember who said what and where, we may miss out on some great teaching and learning opportunities. Now you may be thinking, "With the LDS references in the back and the great search capabilities of most digital versions of the Bible, why even try to remember who said what and where, when you can look it up in seconds?" There are at least two reasons these may not be sufficient. First, regarding digital references—most people don't have their computers, even laptops or a palm pilot, with them when these teaching moments arise. But you are more likely to carry a copy of the scriptures. Or if you are home teaching, the person you are visiting will likely have a Bible handy. However, even with the scriptures or a palm pilot, if you don't know the exact words used in the verse you are looking for, you may have a hard time finding it. If you look up *offense* or *offended*, *golden rule*, or *trinity*, you are not likely to find what you are looking for. Even if you do, it still may take some tedious time checking through the various references to find what you need. So in this chapter we will explore how to create clear, concrete associations so you will always be able to easily remember who said what and where that is found in the New Testament.

Who Said That?

Most books on how to improve your memory have a section on how to remember names and faces. This is important for social graces. However, with regards to remembering what's in the New Testament, we don't have to worry about faces. You can give these characters any face you choose because, of course, no one knows what they really looked like. And remembering most of the relevant names should not be so difficult either. Indeed there are a number of new and somewhat difficult to remember names in the New Testament, but few of them wrote important historical information or provided recorded sermons or said or did other things that are really essential to remember.

It's nice to know that Zacchaeus was the name of the rich publican who climbed the tree to see Jesus. But what's really important is how his faith, devotion, and care for the poor was rewarded, and the parable of the talents that Jesus taught in his house, and where to find that if you needed to teach a lesson on using the gifts God has given us.

If it's not relevant to my salvation, or the salvation and progression of others, or even to understanding the events in the Bible, why bother learning it? We only have so much time on this earth to "prepare to meet God," so I don't usually use my time, nor my limited brainpower, to remember odd names or trivia, even if it is in scriptures. Maybe it will be of use to me someday, and when that day comes, I'll look it up and get it down, but until then there's too much more important information to remember.

Of the names that are important to remember in the New Testament, most of them are household names, names we've known since our youth. You're not going to forget Matthew, Mark, Luke, John, Peter, or Paul. Indeed those are some of the most common names in the English language. Nevertheless, there are a significant number of strange but important names you will want to remember like Zacharias, Nicodemus, Theophilus, Zebedee, Philemon, and so forth. Here are the guidelines for remembering names and tying them to significant lessons, quotes, or events.

1. Make an association. Find some part of the name that you can associate with some person, thing, or action that you are already familiar with. I'll use the name Nicodemus for an example, since that is not a common name, nor does it sounds like anything I'm familiar with. But if we break it down, *Nic* sounds like Nick in Nickel, or Nic in Nicotene, or Nicoderm (a nicotene patch to prevent smoking). *Odemus* reminds me of edema. So to help me remember Nicodemus, I could imagine him with a big nickel, or smoking, or wearing a Nicoderm patch on a swollen (edema) arm. I think I'll choose the latter. (I used to work with people trying to stop smoking so I'm quite familiar with Nicoderm patches. If you are not—and I doubt most active LDS would be—you would not want to use this as a reminder.) So I imagine when Nicodemus comes at night to see Jesus that he is smoking a cigarette. I can see the red glow as he approaches, but before he reaches Jesus, he puts out his cigarette. Then I can now see that his right forearm is very swollen, and he has a patch on it. I also imagine that before the Bible dialogue starts, one of Jesus' disciples asks him why his arm is so swollen, and Nicodemus tells him that he is trying to renew his lungs by stopping smoking and his Nicoderm patch must be causing the edema. One of Jesus' disciples quips, "So we could say Nicoedema is with us, or Nicodem-us for short." (The fact that neither cigarettes nor Nicoderm patches are in the Bible helps me remember that this is simply a memory aid I've thrown in to help me remember the name of the Pharisee Jesus taught about being born again.)

Remember your clue doesn't have to be identical, or even sound identical, to that which you need to remember. You just need a reminder, a hint that is close enough to trigger your natural recall ability. In fact, for this name, since you've likely heard it many times before, just "Nic" or "jolly old St. Nic" would likely be enough to trigger a total recall of his name.

2. Tie to text. Tie the words or phrase used to remember the name to some key phrase or idea you want to remember from the text. In this passage about Nicodemus, the important idea to remember comes from Jesus' statement that "except a man be born again, he cannot see the kingdom of God" (John 3:3). So I might imagine Jesus prefacing these remarks with the comment that if he Nicodemus wants a real renewal, he needs not only a patch but needs to be "born again."

On the other hand, it's more likely that a person would remember the concept of being born again but just not recall the name of the Pharisee Jesus taught that concept to. By remembering this scene with the Pharisee wearing the Nicoderm patch, we will be reminded that his name was Nicodemus.

3. Write it. Jot down the name along with its more memorable picture association. Then next to it or below it, write the quote, concept, or actions from the text that you want to remember that was associated in the text with this person. In this case, we would have written down:

Nicodemus—wearing a Nicoderm patch on a swollen arm with edema. Jesus tells him that a man must be "born again."

4. Periodic Rehearsal. Practice rehearsing the name and connection at spaced intervals. You may want to keep a list of these hard-to-remember names, their reminder picture, person or phrase, and the related text or concepts you want to remember. Then periodically review your list.

One good way to do this would be to use the folded paper techniques. On the outside of the fold you would put the concept or event you want to remember. Then on the inside you would put the name associated with this teaching or event that you find hard to remember. On the other inside fold, you could put the name reminder and link to the text. Then for rehearsal, just pull out the sheet of paper. Fold it so all you can see are the concepts/events. Then from memory try to recall the connection—who said or did that? See the example below:

outside	inside left	inside right
concept, lesson, or quote:	name:	clue:
We must be born again of water and the Spirit.	Nicodemus	Nicodemus is smoking or wears a Nicoderm patch on his swollen (edma) arm.

Again, as with most of the other memory enhancement techniques used here, often all our memory needs is a bit of a hint, and it will be able to take it from there and recall the rest of the story.

I will again illustrate these first three steps, with three names that are difficult to remember: Zacharias, Theophilus, and Beelzebub.

Association: Zacharias—Sack of rye

Concept to remember: He is the husband of Elizabeth and father of John the Baptist

Tied together: I see him carry a sack of rye into the temple. He lays it upon the alter of incense, and an angel appears and tells him that his wife will bear a son who will prepare the way for the coming of the lord

Association: Theophilus—a man of God (Theo) named Phil.

Text to remember: This is the person to whom Luke wrote his gospel and the book of Acts.

Tied together: I see a man I know named Phil, ask Luke to fill him and his friends (us) in on the story of God (Theo) and His work through Jesus and His apostles. He then receives two epistles—the Gospel of Luke and Acts of the Apostles. Since he's such a great believer in God, Luke calls him Theophil.

Association: Beelzebub—a chubby spirit called Bubba for short, wearing bells.

Text to remember: The prince of devils. The Pharisees accuse Jesus of casting out evil spirits through him.

Tied together: I see this chubby demon, Beelzebubba, with bells hanging from his ears that tinkle as he laughs at the Pharisees who accuse Jesus of casting out evil spirits by him.

Caution: You will want to practice these names and connections periodically, or they may fade into oblivion. I know of a man who, after being introduced to a Colonel Hoover, found he could remember the Colonel's name by just imagining him pushing around a Hoover vacuum cleaner. The technique seemed to work the rest of that day, so well in fact that he forgot about it until some weeks later when they met again. Immediately the image of the man pushing the vacuum sprang into memory. Being over-confident and under-rehearsed, he enthusiastically greeted the man by saying, "Well, hello, Colonel Oreck. Nice to see you again." Needless to say, the Colonel was not impressed with his memory.

Where Is That Found?

Since our memories are never perfect, it's usually good to know where various teachings can be found in the New Testament for easy reference. This can also save a lot of time not having to hunt through the index. Even if you know a whole chapter verbatim, it's important to know the gospel or epistle it is in as well as the chapter number, in case you quote something that your listener would later like to look up. First let's discuss how to link the text to the right book or epistle and then to the right chapter.

Now that you have learned how to remember names, it should not be difficult to develop a picture or person to associate with each gospel or epistle. Indeed we have already done this in the previous chapter. When you think of the gospel of Matthew, that should bring someone to mind named Matt. The same is true with Mark, Luke, John, and the epistles sent to individuals. The same principle applies to the other epistles written by apostles, namely James, John, Peter, and Jude. You can avoid confusion between the gospel of John and the epistles of John by imagining them in different settings, or I would imagine the epistles being written or told to me by a much older John with a long beard. For the book of Acts, I imagine Theophilus with sunglasses on—looking like an actor. For Romans, I associate a Roman soldier; Corinthians, someone with an apple core; Galatians, a woman in western attire—a gal; Ephesians, men with their hands out asking for a fee; Philippians, flipping coins; Colossians closing their windows; Thessalonians with thistles; and so on. You will likely have your own images representing these different books, that you developed in chapter 5.

Now you just need to associate the appropriate book with its selected content. If you are remembering something from the gospel of Matthew, you could think of your friend Matt telling you this, or imagine him in the picture writing, or otherwise present as you imagine that scene. He would be with the shepherds when the angel sang at Bethlehem when the wise men came, and at the Sermon on the Mount. Or you should be able to imagine him telling you about these. Accordingly, Theophilus, the actor, would tell you about the day of Pentecost, or be present in the picture as you visualized that event. Corinthians could be seen throwing apple cores and contending with one another resulting in Paul's stern words regarding divisions not being of God. You could see a second group with half-eaten apples (cores) being taught about the law of witnesses in 2 Corinthians 13, a woman with a western hat (a gal) in the picture with the fruit of the Spirit (see Galatians 5:22), a Hebrew slave being told about the Father of Spirits (see Hebrews 12:9), and so on.

Several systems have been developed to help people remember numbers. These can easily be adapted for remembering page and chapter numbers, as well as the contents of these chapters or pages. Personally, I prefer to remember chapter numbers since there are fewer of them than pages in the New Testament and because not all Bibles, especially electronic editions, have the same page numbering system. But they do have the same chapter divisions.

A Bit of History

The Numerical Order Alphabet, as it is called, goes back to at least 1648 when Stanislaus Mink von Wennsshein first introduced the concept. Dr. Richard Grey expanded on it in 1730. In 1886, A. S. Boyd in "The World's Important Facts and How to Remember Them," 5th Edition, mentions that earlier in that century Professor Pliny Miles delivered lectures which described this system. In 1890 William James included it in his "Principles of Psychology." In this system, since numbers are abstractions that can be hard to remember, each number 0–9 was assigned a phonetic sound (as in Hebrew these are all consonant sounds). Then easily imagined words, made from these sounds, were assigned to each number. The original system consisted of 100 picture words representing the numbers 1–100. Most modern memory performers or mnemonists use this or a similar system. We will use a similar system here. Many of the picture words have been changed or adapted to make them more concrete and contemporary, but the underlying phonetic numbering system has remained the same. What follows are the numbers 0–9 with their corresponding phonetic sounds (read these as sounds rather than as letters).

0	1	2	3	4	5	6	7	8	9
s	t	n	m	r	L	sh	k	f	p
c	d					j	g	v	b
z						ch	c (hard)		

By saying each letter associated with each number, you will soon be able to pick up the associated sounds. The system is rather simple, and as you will soon see, ingenious. But just to clarify—for 6 the sound is a soft "sh" as in shoe, or j as in judge, or ch as in church. You could also use g as in gym. For 7 the sound is a hard "k" as in key, or g as in gate, or c as in cash (you will note this "c" has more of a "k" sound, and is a much different sound than the "ch" in church).

Note: If you run through them a few times, you will find them easy to remember. But you can also find an easy method for remembering this phonetic numbering system with its associated "peg" words at the end of this chapter. However, you don't even need to remember these, as long as you can remember the picture words that go with each number listed below.

Once these basic sounds are firmly associated in your brain with their corresponding number, it's relatively easy to come up with words to represent larger numbers, especially two digit numbers. For example, to represent the number 12, you could use the words TiN, TeeN, ToNe, TuNe, TaN, DaN, DoNe, DuNe, DiNe, or DeN. For my purposes I usually use the word TiN—and picture a TiN can. I've selected "tin can" because it is a concrete familiar object that can easily be put into motion and linked (related/associated) with other objects with a little action—a swift kick. Now let's see how these principles can work together with this system to create memorable images, linking chapter numbers to text content.

To illustrate, the first chapter 12 in the New Testament is of course Matthew 12. This chapter opens with the Pharisees questioning Jesus about His disciples gleaning and eating ears of corn on the Sabbath. To link this story with the number 12, I imagine one of the Pharisees kicking a big tin can into a corn field as he and his cohorts approached Jesus and his disciples, picking corn. The can hits a friend of mine named Matt in the shin, while he is standing with Jesus picking corn. He looks up and asks, "What was that?" Well, actually it was just a little reminder that this Sabbath scene takes place in Matthew chapter 12. The rest of the scenes and events in chapter 12 can be linked together from there, using the methods you learned in chapters 5, as well as those we will explore in chapters 7 and 9. So when you think of any event from chapter 12, it can lead you back to the memory peg for that chapter, which in this case is—TiN can—representing chapter 12.

Note: the picture words used for numbers are often referred to as "peg words" or "memory pegs," because like pegs on a wall or hat stand, you can "hang" or "attach" other new, less common or less memorable items or images to them. So these of necessity must be easily remembered words, words that are concrete or represent objects that are easy to picture.

Now lets review the entire primary number peg list. This list was developed from several others and a few of my own inventions. Feel free to substitute or add your own peg words. You may be able to come up with others that have the requisite consonant sounds that are easier for you to remember. (For a great list of options for numbers 1–100, see BYU professor Kenneth Higbee's *Your Memory: How It Works and How to Improve It,* cited in "Sources" at the end of this book.)

This list contains picture words that for me are familiar, concrete, easily imagined, or conducive to action images. In most cases, these are modern or unusual words for that setting and so not easily confused with other things in the New Testament.

Number pegs/objects for remembering chapters in the New Testament:

1. tie
2. snow
3. mow (lawn mower)
4. row, oar
5. law (sheriff)
6. shoe
7. key
8. sofa
9. pie
10. toes
11. toad
12. tin (can or cup)
13. tomb (open grave)
14. tire
15. towel
16. dish
17. tack
18. TV
19. tub
20. noose, news (newspaper)
21. net
22. nun
23. name (nameplate hung on a chain)
24. Nero (fiddling)
25. nail
26. nudge
27. knock
28. knife
29. nap (hammock)
30. moss, Moose
31. mitt (baseball mitt)
32. man (man in black)
33. Mom (my mom)
34. hammer
35. mail (mailman or letters)
36. match (that you strike)
37. mike (as in microphone)
38. movie
39. mop
40. rose
41. radio
42. horn (Bugle)
43. ram (Dodge truck)
44. rear (horse rear up)
45. reel
46. rash
47. rake
48. roof
49. rope
50. light (flashlight)
51. lid
52. lion
53. llama
54. lure (used for fishing)
55. lolly-pop (lollipop)
56. leach
57. lick
58. loaf (loaf of bread)
59. lap (laptop computer)
60. jazz (saxophone)
61. shot (with a needle)
62. shin (kick in the)
63. jam
64. chair
65. Jello
66. judge (gavel)
67. shock
68. shave (as with a razor)
69. jeep
70. gauze (bandages)
71. kite
72. cane
73. comb
74. crow
75. coal
76. cage
77. gag
78. coffee
79. cape
80. fuse
81. photo (snapping a photo)
82. fan
83. foam
84. fur
85. foil (wrapped in tin foil)
86. effigy (hung on a rope)
87. fig or fog
88. five
89. VIP
90. pizza
91. bat
92. piano
93. bomb
94. bury
95. bell
96. pitch (pitch a soft ball)
97. pack (back pack)
98. pave (as in pave the road)
99. pipe
100. daisies

Practice going over these on a regular basis to keep them fresh in your memory, at least the first thirty until you've used them a number of times in the New Testament. After that, they will be easier to remember. But if you ever forget a word, just sound out the sounds representing the number you want, and the peg word should soon come to you.

Using the System to Teach a Lesson

Now, let's see how this system could be used to help a person you know who has a problem letting go of past offenses. For illustration purposes, let's say this person tells you that he does not intend to come back to church as long as your current bishop is still the bishop there because of certain things that the bishop has said in the past that were offensive to him. You ask your friend if he still believes in Jesus Christ and the Bible to be the word of God. He affirms that he does. As he tells you about this offense and his feelings, a couple of scriptures come to mind. But you can't remember for sure what they say, nor can you recall where they are found. That evening you resolve to find those scriptures and commit their location to memory so that next time you encounter a person who needs to be more forgiving, you can share with them the counsel of Christ on this subject.

The scripture that comes to mind is Jesus' counsel on forgiveness and the importance of going to the person in private who has offended you. In the same chapter, He talks about how many times we should be willing to forgive, and then He tells a story about a man who owed his lord a large debt. In his final statement in that chapter, He notes, "And his lord was wroth [because he would not forgive another], and delivered him to the tormentors, till he should pay all that was due unto him. So likewise shall my heavenly Father do also unto you, if ye from your hearts forgive not every one his brother their trespasses."

With a bit of searching, you would find that this is in chapter 18 of Matthew. Then if you've been practicing the peg list, you will remember that the peg or picture word for 18 is TV. To make the connection, you could imagine the person you know named Matthew telling you about a man who took a big screen TV from the lord of the manor without paying for it. And then you could put yourself into the story and imagine a servant of the lord confronting him in private. Once caught, he begs (on his knees with his clasped hands on the TV) for forgiveness. The TV reminds you that this story about forgiveness is in chapter 18. Again, obviously the part about the TV is not part of the actual story but is a memory device to help you remember the location of this teaching on forgiveness.

A few reviews of this scene with a man asking forgiveness for a debt incurred by a big TV and that concept with its location will be firmly fixed in your memory for ready recall the next time an opportunity arises.

Important Cautions and Tips When Using Number Pegs

There is a danger in using a peg system or introducing artificial elements into the New Testament story to facilitate recall. If you are not careful, it may become difficult later on to distinguish between the original elements of the text and the foreign aids to memory. Therefore, when developing my pegs and pictures, there are a number of things I've learned to do in order to help me keep these separate in my mind.

1. You will note that very few of my peg words or images are used elsewhere in the New Testament (there are no tins cans or TVs in the text), nor are they objects, symbols, or actions that would be common to normal Jewish activities. In fact, most of them like Tie-1, TiN-12, and TiRe-14 are objects that were not invented until after the New Testament was written. So if I see one of those in a scene I've created in my mind, I know that this represents the chapter number.

2. When I imagine these number pegs or symbols, if they could have an old world setting, I imagine a modern version, like

an electric carving kNiFe for 28, or RaM truck for 43; or I imagine them being red in color. For example, if I use NeT to remember the number 21, or NaiL to remember 25, I will imagine a red net or a red nail. Thus they are truly "extraordinary," and so, as noted above, more memorable.

3. I am careful not to make these features more prominent in my story line or mental movie than the original text or message elements.

These three steps, used together, help to prevent a mix-up or confusion between the artificial memory devices and the message or concepts found in the Bible. So if you use a red peg picture word in a scene you envision, you should be able to easily distinguish later the peg or number object from the original text.

While there are often many word options for each number, it's usually best to use a standard list like the one provided above. And when a number has more than one peg word option, select only one word to use so that each number is always represented by the same word picture. If you come up with other peg words that work better for you, go with those. Just don't try to use more than one in the same book or project. Otherwise it could become confusing. And that brings us to another question.

Will the Pictures Become Confused?

Some people wonder, if they use these same peg picture words over and over to represent the chapters of each book of the New Testament, won't that become confusing? Not usually. The reason is, each book provides a different setting for that picture or object. For example, each of the four gospels has a chapter 3. In fact, every book in the New Testament has a chapter 3 (except the last two epistles of John and Jude). The peg word for 3 is *mow*. So I could imagine a lawn mower associated with the events in each chapter 3. But because each setting is different and the writer or receiver are different, they should not get confused. Everyone in your neighborhood likely has a lawn mower, but I doubt you would confuse yours with theirs. The exceptions to this are the books of Matthew and Luke. Chapter 3 in both of those books talks about the same events—the preaching of John and the baptism of Jesus. So you could imagine both Matthew and Luke standing by the river Jordan leaning on the handles of two lawn mowers, and then you would remember that both of them talk about this event in chapter 3 of their gospels, albeit each a bit differently. That shouldn't be confusing. In fact, it would make for easy cross referencing.

How Can You Remember Verse Locations?

Personally I do not use this system to remember the location of every verse. That would introduce too many foreign elements into the text and perhaps lead to distortions in the message. While it is possible to use two separate peg lists (and actually I'll share another one below), tying picture words from two systems into one text would be too complex and distracting, at least for me. I've found that most people have either marked their scriptures so as to be able to easily find their favorite texts in a chapter, or they can usually see in their mind's eye the order or location of concepts within a chapter. Plus, as you will see in chapters 7 and 9, if you commit to memory a chapter at a time, the concepts (at least the ones most important to you) will be linked together in sequential order. So at least you will know if the concept or verse you are looking for comes at the first or last of the chapter. Then too in the scriptures you can always look at the chapter summaries at the beginning of each chapter for a clue.

Having said that, there are many verses that you will likely want to remember the specific location for. In order to do this, there are at least three techniques you can use. First, you can use this same number system, but give the objects representing the verses a different color, say green. Let's take Matthew 18 verse 15 for example. It reads, "Moreover if thy brother shall trespass against thee, go and tell him his fault between thee and him alone: if he shall hear thee, thou hast gained thy brother."

If you look on the chart, you will see that the peg word used to represent the number 15 is *towel*. So you could imagine that when the servant comes to confront the man with his debt, that he has around his neck a large bright green towel, which I would also imagine the debtor using to wipe the sweat from his brow, as the magnitude of his TV debt is revealed in private. The green towel would remind you this is in verse 15.

Second, you could also use the alternative rhyming system mentioned below or some other system. This is not as convenient, however, for remembering numbers larger than 10. If I were to use this system to remember locations in the New Testament, I would use it to remember the chapter numbers, since they do not go as high as the verse numbers. (I'll explain below how to use this for numbers greater than 10.) Several of the epistles have fewer than 10 chapters. I would then use the primary phonetic system to peg the desired verses.

Third, you could do what most do, and that is just do a lot of practice rehearsals using these verses with their numbers so that when you recite the specific scripture you give the specific verse with it, thus more closely associating the two together in memory. With this verse, for example, you would say, "Matthew 18 verse 15: Moreover, if thy brother shall trespass against thee . . . "

How to Remember the Phonetic System and Its Peg Words

In this short section, I will share with you two different ways to remember this phonetic numbering system. First, to simply remember the sounds associated with each number, just think of the following parts of your body, in order, from bottom to top.

0. Sole (of your feet) gives the "s" sound.	6. Chest and shoulder give you "ch" and "sh" sounds.
1. Toes give you the "t" sound.	7. Collar bone give you the "k" sound.
2. Knee gives you the "n" sound.	8. Face gives you the "f" sound.
3. Thigh Muscle gives you the "m" sound.	9. Pate (top of head) gives you the "p" sound.
4. Rear end gives you the "r" sound.	
5. Love handles give you the "l" sound.	

Now go through these and touch each body part as you say the associated sound. Do it three times today and three times tomorrow, and you'll soon have these sounds down. But these really are not as important to learn as the first ten picture words. If you can remember them, they will also remind you of the ten phonetic sounds. Here is an easy way to remember them.

The letter "t" in "tie" looks like the number 1. Then the next three words rhyme—snow, mow, and row. Law is just one vowel sound from low, which would rhyme with row, and a law man's badge has 5 points. A shoe hanger looks like a 6. The number 7 is a "key" number in the Old Testament. The script ƒ – the main consonant sound in sofa, looks like the number 8. The "p" in pie is a 9 in reverse. Toes, the word for 10, is easy. You have 10 of them.

If that is not enough to help you remember the first ten peg words, I suggest you link them together like this. See yourself coming out of your house fixing your **tie**, and it's **sNow**ing, but you can still see your neighbor **Mow**ing his lawn, and someone **Row**ing by in a row boat. A **Law** man stops them and tells them no rowing on pavement. That is what a **SHoe** is for, to walk on pavement. You decide this whole scene is too crazy for you, so you decide to go back inside, but now you've locked the door and so have to fumble for your **Key**. Once inside you flop down on your **soFa**, and begin to eat your favorite **Pie**. Soon you are asleep snoring **zzz's**, the sound for 0. Can you see that? Perhaps you can make up an even better story to remember these sounds.

The Rhyming Number Memory Systems

Since this need to recall the location of important text is as old as books, it's no wonder there have been several systems developed to help people remember numbers in general and page or chapter numbers in particular, as well as how to mentally tie these effectively to the contents or concepts on those pages.

One other system I like is the rhyming system. This system has paired words that rhyme with each number. One form is as follows.

1. one—gun, or mon-ey
2. two—shoe
3. three—tree
4. four—door
5. five—hive (bee)
6. six—sticks
7. seven—heaven (I picture a garden)
8. eight—gate
9. nine—dine
10. ten—hen

It's nice to have this second system as well to help remember numbered items within a text, especially when the items number 10 or less. You can also use this system to remember higher numbers. In that case, you would just need to add the symbols. For example, for the number 13 you would imagine a gun and a tree. For 24 you would picture a shoe and a door. But of course, the phonetic numbering system is simpler for larger numbers (you only have to pair one object instead of two), and that is why I use it as my primary system to remember chapters and verses when needed.

An obvious use for this rhyming system to 10 would be to help you remember the 10 commandments in order and the number that goes with each. If someone said, "He broke the sixth commandment," you'd know what sort of offender you were dealing with.

Now that you understand the peg system and how it works, as well as how to make strong, memorable associations, let's practice using this rhyming system with the Ten Commandments. I've provided the peg symbols and each commandment (leaving off the "Thou shalts") in order. All you need to do is make up a memorable picture to tie them together and write that out to the side, or on a separate sheet of paper. Note: you will need to come up with your own images/symbols to represent the pegs. Just be creative and have some fun.

1. Gun—no other gods before me.
2. Shoe—Not make unto thee any graven image.
3. Tree—Not take the name of the Lord thy God in vain.
4. Door—Remember the Sabbath day, to keep it holy.
5. Hive—Honor thy father and thy mother.
6. Sticks—Not kill.
7. Heaven—Not commit adultery.
8. Gate—Not steal.
9. Dine—Not bear false witness against thy neighbor.
10. Hen—Not covet.

This system can also be used as a substitute for the link system to remember the different points made in a talk. With that method, you would relate each concept taught to one of these number pegs in order (a gun with their first point, a shoe with the second, a tree with the third, and so on). Few speakers will ever try to make more than ten different points in the same address.

A Bonus Benefit for Those Who Persist

In the next chapter we will review another great way to organize and remember what you read or hear in conference. But first, here's one important, encouraging note about the peg system and your memory. This system may seem a bit complicated and initially intimidating. However, if you persist in taking the time to learn the peg system and use it to remember chapter locations and content, in time this will become much easier, and the peg words second nature, or synonymous with their associated numbers. And then if you continue to practice these associations (recalling the location of various stories and events via the peg system—in effect over-learning these), you will find that you no longer even have to think of the peg word; you will just automatically remember the location of each event or teaching. At least that is what I have found, and others who have used this system have reported similar results. But initially this system is a great way to help a person remember who said what, where, with phenomenal results almost immediately. And it can be a lot of fun!

For more information regarding the peg number system and examples of its use in remembering the location of scriptures, go to www.ARECORD4LDS.com.

7

MEMORY MAPPING

Many years ago, I signed up for Evelyn Wood's Reading Dynamics speed reading program. Developed by Mrs. Wood at the University of Utah in the mid 1960s, it is still advertised as "the world's foremost reading improvement and study skills course."[1] Among her students were many high level people in business and government, including John F. Kennedy. The methods she developed enabled her students to read more than 2000 words per minute with good comprehension. One of her key techniques for long-term retention was an innovative method for note-taking, which she called recall patterns. In a later book on these methods,

Stanley D. Frank, EdD, executive vice-president of Encyclopedia Britannica, noted, "The best way to enable yourself to remember and use these materials [what you study] is to take notes."[2]

Their methods for taking notes, however, were unconventional. Just copying down words requires little mental involvement and so, although helpful, it is of limited value for retention. Therefore, Evelyn Wood and her instructors developed a much more active process for note-taking. The recall patterns that they developed did not look like traditional notes—written horizontally in a linear outline. Instead, they looked more like diagrams, trees, fishbones, or flow charts. Here are two examples:

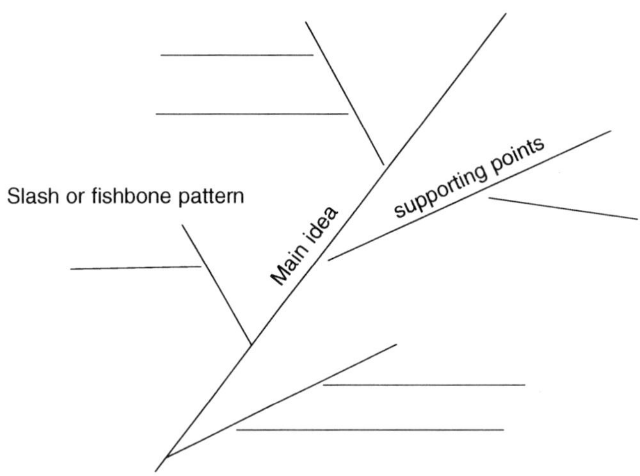

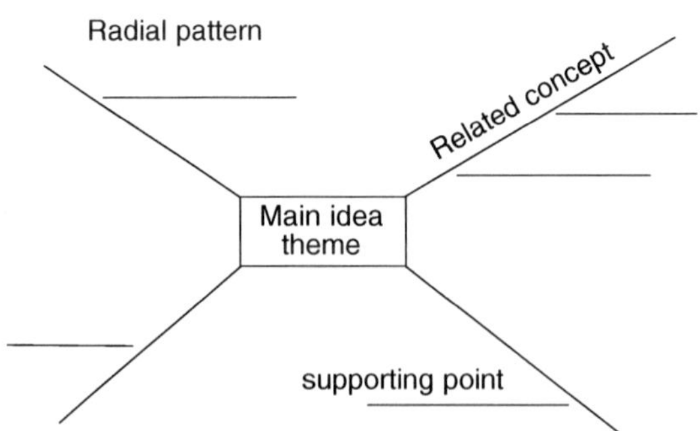

As you can see, in each of these, the main idea is in the center. It's either written along the center line, usually vertically slanted or noted within a geometrical shape in or near the center. Additional related or supporting concepts and ideas branch out from there, each with their own supporting points.

These diagrams may require a bit more effort, attention, and organizing to develop than a traditional outline. However, as a result, they are easier to remember. Actually, there are three primary reasons they turn out to be more memorable than traditional outlines. (We will discuss additional reasons later in this chapter.) We have already mentioned two of these.

First, they require us to pay closer attention and get more involved with the material. Second, the concepts are interrelated and organized in ways you chose, thus making it more memorable than if you were just to use someone else's organization. And third, in the process, you create a visual image of your own making. Such unusual pictures, arranged in unique ways, are much easier to recall than uniform lines of letters alone. Plus, as with any type of writing, you will remember better what you graphically put to paper than what someone else has.

Because they do take extra time and effort to develop, you wouldn't want to use these with everything that you read or hear. However, when you come to something that you feel is really important to remember, the returns you will achieve with this system, in improved storage and recall ability, more than make up for the extra time and effort this may require.

Mind Mapping

In the decade that followed the advent of Evelyn Wood's reading dynamics and recall patterns, another educator, Tony Buzan, developed a similar system in England for note taking and remembering. He called his system mind mapping. Buzan observed that the way the brain actually functions is not congruent with traditional outlines. Instead it tends to make connections in various directions. It's no wonder, therefore, and no accident, that the "mind maps" which he and his students later developed look much like the structure of a nervous system or memory itself, with a large cell or "neuron" in the middle and its "axons" (large branches) and their smaller "dendrites" branching out from there. Below is a typical "mind map." As you can see, this is actually on the process of mind mapping, taken with permission from a Buzan "preferred partner" Web page.

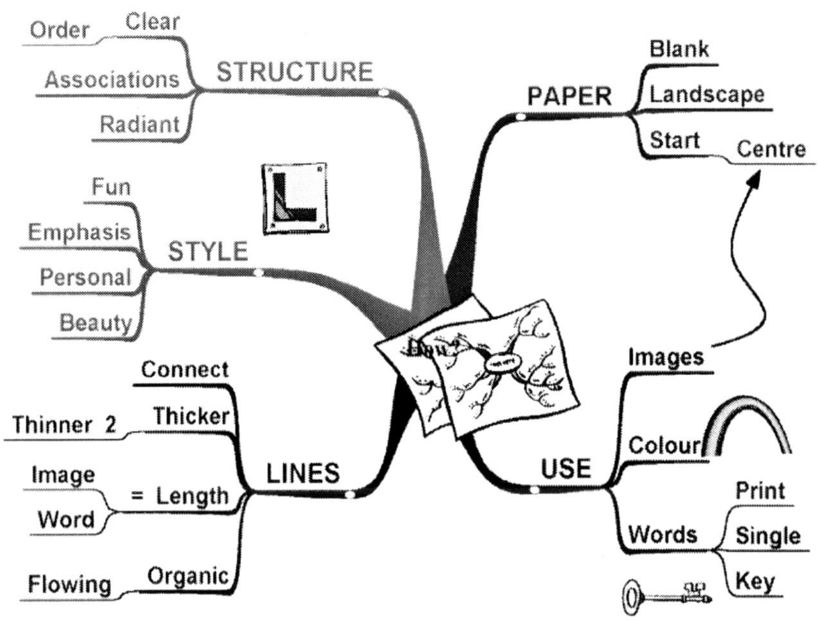

(In case you are wondering what the "L" is for, in England those who are first learning how to drive are required to have an "L" sign displayed on their car to show others that they are just "learning." And of course, mind mapping is all about helping us to learn.)

The original and additional examples for various uses can be found at www.mind-mapping.co.uk/mind-maps-examples.htm. Note: Although this is in black and white, in the original, each branch has its own color. Buzan believed it easier to remember that way.

Since mind mapping, or what I like to call memory mapping, was developed in the late 1970s, it has been used by students of all ages and at all levels with dramatic results. Below is an explanation of how mind maps are made.

1. You will need a blank piece of paper, at least letter size (legal may be better).

2. Place the paper on a good writing surface in landscape orientation so you have more space to write from left to right.

3. Start in the center, with a word or two that represents the central idea of the chapter or talk you are taking notes on.

4. Draw an image or symbol near or around these center words to represent the main topic. (Buzan suggests coloring this, using at least three colors.)

- Keep the height and width of the central image relatively small, approximately one to two inches (proportionately larger for bigger paper). This size gives plenty of space for the rest of your map, while making it large enough to be the center of attention.
- Allow the image to create its own shape.
- A picture is worth a thousand words. It opens up associations, focuses the thoughts, is fun, and results in better recall.
- Using color stimulates the right cortical activity of imagination as well as capturing and holding attention.
- The unique shape makes it more memorable and enjoyable.

5. Note the main supporting themes or idea on branches radiating from the central image.

- Print these words in CAPITALS or draw an image.
- These lines are thicker, curved, and naturally flowing like an arm extending from the body, or the branch of a tree from the trunk.

6. These main themes, connected to the central image, are the Basic Ordering Ideas (BOIs) and organize and focus the rest of the mind map.

• Print, rather than cursive script, is easier for most to see and remember.

• Word length equals line length.

• Curved lines give visual variety and so are easier to remember, more pleasant to draw, and less boring to look at. Thicker central lines show relative importance.

7. The next level of words or images are linked to the main branch that triggered them. Words are still printed but may be lower case.

• Connected lines create relationships and structure. They also demonstrate the level of importance, as from a branch to a twig.

• The size and style of the letters provide additional data about the importance and meaning of the word/image.

8. Add a third or fourth level of data, depending on how much detail you want to remember. But keep in mind, it's easier to remember fewer words. So focus on the key concepts and data that would be most important to remember.

• Use images as much as you can, instead of, or in addition to, the words.

• You can "jump about" the mind map, adding additional ideas and connecting associations as they are presented.

9. Add boxes or other shapes around key words or images to make the most important points stand out.

10. You may also want to enclose branches of a mind map with outlines in color.

These outlines can have unique shapes, as you might find in clouds, and may make it easier to recall. You can also show connections by using the same color for different but related branches.

Additionally, proponents suggest that if you put some effort into making your mind maps artistic, colorful, imaginative, distinctive, and multi-dimensional, your eyes and brain will be more attracted to them and they will be easier to remember.

They also encourage mappers to have fun. Add a little humor or exaggeration, and your brain will delight in getting the maximum use and enjoyment from this process and will therefore learn faster, recall more effectively, and think more clearly.

Studying with Maps in Mind

Now that you have the basics of what I like to call memory mapping, let's discuss how this process can be used to help you better remember what you read in the scriptures or hear in conference. Before doing so, however, I want to review one other system for study. This is called the SQ4R method and has been taught in study skills classes at most universities in the United States.

The letters SQ4R stand for Survey, Question, Read, wRite, Recite, and Review. Studies that led to the development of SQ4R showed that people were able to retain more of their reading if they first did a quick Survey of the material to get the main idea and then formulated a few Questions to ask themselves as they read it through. Then of course they would Read it to find the answers to their questions; wRite down their answers; practice Reciting the answers; and then at the end, Review what they had learned. As with the other diagramming or mapping techniques outlined above, you may not always, or even often, have time to use this approach. Indeed it wouldn't seem practical for casual reading, but when you find a chapter that is particularly insightful or full of great wisdom that you would want to pass on to others, then you may want to use this approach.

The following are specific steps adapted from these two learning strategies—SQ4R and mind mapping—steps that you may want to consider to increase your comprehension and recollection of what you read in the New Testament.

1. Look at the summaries at the beginning of each chapter. Quickly browse or look through the chapter or chapters you intend to read in this sitting. This process should give you the main theme for a central image and main branches (or basic Ordering Ideas) for your map of the text.

2. Map out or diagram the main ideas that you picked up from your preview.

3. Formulate questions to be answered as you read more carefully.

4. Read the selection answering the questions, highlighting or circling the most important words, and adding other important details to your map as you go. Check the footnotes for clarification.

5. Finally there is the review stage in which you look back over the text to answer any remaining questions or clarify any parts that are not well understood. You may want to check out a few cross-references. Then complete your map notes, coloring or otherwise highlighting the most important ideas to remember.

In chapter 9 we will review a more comprehensive plan for committing what we read to memory, combining mapping methods with techniques taught in previous chapters. However, at this point, please keep in mind that if you really want to make sure your memory map makes it into long-term storage, you will need to do some periodic review without looking at the map. One method is to simply redraw your map from memory, as much as you can, and then check and fill in what you missed. The repetition will greatly increase your recall ability.

Adaptations for Conference Talks

Mapping is also a great way to help us remember what we hear in general conference. Listening to a speaker is a pretty passive activity, and unless we employ some other strategies, we will forget most of what we hear. By taking notes or mapping what you hear, you should be able to at least double the amount that you remember.

Of course, the five steps noted above for reading would not be applicable when listening to a message. In that case, you would simply start by writing down, in a box or circle near the middle of your page, what appears to be the main topic. This is usually stated within the first minute of a formal address. Sometimes the speaker will tell a joke or story to get people's attention, but then they will usually state their topic or purpose. From there you can begin to develop your branches with supporting ideas. Of course, you would start a new branch in a different direction each time the speaker makes a new point, with supporting information branching off from the main points or ideas. Don't worry if you don't get it perfect. You can re-write it or draw connecting lines later. The important thing is that you write down the most helpful ideas that you hear. That activity alone will force you to pay closer attention. It will also keep you awake. And when combined with the visual picture you create, this simple process can greatly increase your retention. And of course, once it's down on paper, you can easily review or rehearse what you wrote to strengthen those cerebral connections.

Computerized Maps

If you really get into this and would prefer cleaner, neater drawings, there is software available that will enable you to develop these maps on your computer. I downloaded a trial version from MindJet at www.mindjet.com/us/solutions/education/. After a bit of practice, I developed the following map of Elder Wolfgang H. Paul's April 2006 conference address on agency.

There is one important thing to keep in mind with memory maps, however. They are very limited reminders of the full content. I was reminded of that recently as I went back to look at Elder Paul's address. While my map does contain most of the

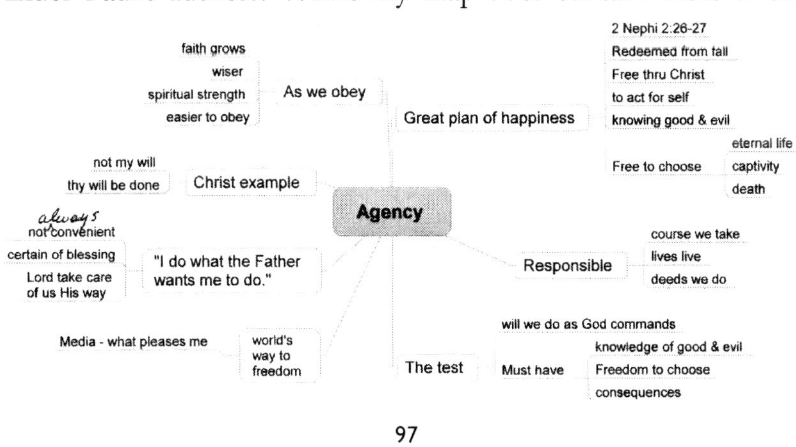

main ideas, I found other important points, quotes, and details that were not adequately captured in my map. It's much better than a plain outline or nothing, but it's best to use this in conjunction with the original highlighted text if you want to remember all of the important content. In fact, a nice test and review for yourself after you have developed a map is to go back and see how much of the original text or details you can recall from just what you have on your map.

Pros and Cons

I found the software fun, and after a bit of practice, relatively easy to use. It makes it simple to add new ideas or lines of thinking and to change things around. You can also type in key quotes if you'd like. It can be useful for developing a lesson or presentation or for brainstorming and creative problem solving. In fact, that is likely its main commercial use. However, these can be developed freehand for those purposes nearly as well, though not as neat. And with a digital version, you can drop it into a Microsoft Word document or PowerPoint for formal presentations.

On the downside, it does take more time than freehand, and the lines won't always go where you want them to go. With the thin, straight lines, the computerized version is not as unique and artistic and therefore may not be quite as memorable as a map that is drawn. You can add pictures from databases to the software version, but of course that would take more time to find what you need than simply drawing them yourself.

In Conclusion

Whatever methods you use for taking notes, whether you use diagrams, recall patterns, mind maps, simple pictures, a traditional outline, or a combination of the above, you will likely remember the material much better than if you did not use one of these graphic aids. And likely the more graphic or picturesque your notes are, the more memorable they will be. The simple act of writing or drawing what you have read will force you to pay closer attention, involve other senses, and leave you something concrete and simpler to review and rehearse. It will take you a bit more time, but the rewards in improved retention and ease of recall will be well worth the effort.

For additional information and examples of memory maps used in remembering the New Testament, go to www.ARECORD4LDS.com.

Notes

1. As advertised on www.evelynwood.com.au/. This site is from Australia. Type Evelyn Wood in your web browser and you will see how popular this course still is around the world.

2. Stanley D. Frank, *Remember Everything You Read: The Evelyn Wood 7 Day Speed Reading and Learning Program*. New York: Times Books, 1990, 109.

8

HOW TO MEMORIZE

Some of the General Authorities, I've noticed, have amazing memories. One of these is Vaughan J. Featherstone, now emeritus. He is especially well known for his ability to recite lengthy poetry. I had an opportunity to talk with Elder Featherstone and asked him how he did it. How was he able to memorize so much? Was it just a gift of the Spirit? He told me it wasn't easy for him. He had to practice over and over. Nearly every night before he went to sleep, he would rehearse in his mind a poem.

Memorization for most people is a real challenge, at least memorizing biblical verses word for word. On the other hand, it can be one of the most useful and rewarding memory feats you can achieve. Nevertheless, as with Elder Featherstone, it usually does take some extra effort and rehearsal.

I am both good and bad at this. I say, "good" because I have memorized several lengthy poems and literally dozens, if not hundreds, of verses of scriptures. I have memorized some with seemingly no effort at all, like Proverbs 3:5 and Doctrine and Covenants 112:10. My parents quoted these to me often and early in life, and these scriptures just got stuck in my memory. On the other hand, generally I find now, when I try to memorize something extensive, it takes some planning, time, and effort. But at least I've learned some methods that do make it a lot easier than it otherwise would be. I will share those methods with you in this chapter. But first, let me introduce you to two people who have made some interesting discoveries along this line.

The first is my son-in-law Larry. Larry has a truly amazing memory for almost everything, everything except lyrics and text, that is. Larry can remember the games he played in nursery. He can even remember his mother pinning on his diaper. That is truly extraordinary. Most people cannot remember anything before their third or fourth birthday.

As a computer programmer, Larry can remember, coordinate, and integrate dozens of lines of programming language on two screens at once. He's an accomplished musician and can play four or five instruments all by ear—but not at the same time, of course! He does have some limitations.

He also knows dozens, if not hundreds, of musical arrangements by heart. He can even listen to a concert and pick out the music of each of the instruments. However, what he cannot do well is remember lyrics. He claims his brain gets so into the music that he cannot focus on or remember the words. He also struggles with memorization of text of any significant length. But being a bright guy, he has figured out ways to overcome this challenge.

Not-So-Vain Repetition

For many years, Larry avoided memorizing words because it was difficult for him. Indeed he feels he developed a mental block against memorization. And when he was forced to, like when he had to memorize the lyrics of a new song for his band, he did it purely by rote (repeating it over and over), but it took him an inordinate amount of time. Then, he started studying artificial intelligence and gained new insight into how the brain works. He reasoned that if computers could learn by having material repeated over and over, he must be able to do this as well.

His basic method, after that, did not change a great deal. He continued to memorize by rote, repeating the material over and over. He would learn a small chunk, and then add a bit more, repeat the whole thing, add a bit more, repeat all of that, add a bit more, and so on. But he found that he was now able to pick up the lyrics and retain them much faster. Why? Because once he realized that if a computer could learn through repetition, then his brain must also be able to pick up more than he had previously thought.

Larry had learned that there was such a thing as un-vain repetition. In other words, he realized his repetition was not in vain. It was, in fact, producing tangible results. Consequently he began to trust his memory more, "that it was getting this information." The more he trusted it, the better it got.

His experience reminds me of the admonition in Doctrine and Covenants, section 88, to "seek learning, even by study and also by faith" (v. 118). It's important, as my son-in-law learned, for us to trust and have faith in the ability of our memories. If you think you can't memorize, you probably will have a difficult time, but if you have faith and expect your brain to deliver, it usually will.

This is reminiscent of the old adage, "If you think you can do a thing or think you can't do a thing, you're right."

John Memorizes the Sermon on the Mount

A good friend of mine has played the part of Jesus in various productions. More recently, he decided to perform the entire Sermon on the Mount. He told me that this was much harder for him than playing a role in a play, where you can cue off other actors to help you remember your lines. In this extraordinary feat of memory, John learned three chapters—more than four pages of text—which took more than thirty minutes to deliver nonstop. If you don't think that is a lot, try it some time. One of the things that makes this even more amazing is that John has a learning disability (dyslexia) that makes it hard for him to read and retain what he's read.

I asked John how he did it. He acknowledged that it wasn't an easy task; it had taken him many months. But he learned several things in the process that made it easier as he went along. He just wished he had known those things in the beginning because it would have saved him some time. I think you'll find his methodology insightful. As you read through his process, you may want to jot down the various principles and techniques he used that we have already discussed, in addition to any new ones that you see. At the end we can compare notes.

First, John read the text over and over. (See his notes and mine below on a better, faster way to begin.)

Second, he meticulously recorded on audio tape every verse, phrase by phrase, making sure he had just the right emphasis and inflection in his voice. He wanted to make sure he had a good audio copy of the text, just as he wanted it delivered, without errors. He recorded this four times onto a single tape, twice on the front side and twice on the back.

Third, he played the tape on a tape player that played continuously, automatically switching from one side to the other. He just turned it on and let it play in the background throughout the day as he pursued other normal activities.

Fourth, he wrote down as much of the text as he could from memory. He wrote it over and over again. He later told me that for him, this was very helpful to drive those lines deep into his memory.

At places where he got stuck, he would write out a key phrase to begin the next thought, like "blessed," to help him remember the beatitudes. Then we wrote out each of these blessed statements:

- Blessed are the poor in spirit.
- Blessed are they that mourn.
- Blessed are the meek.

He would first write and then read and recite each phrase fully. Then he would block out some of the details and try to recite the same thing again.

Fifth, he drew some cues or icons for himself, first in the text, and then in sequential order on a separate sheet of paper. These were picture cues to remind him of the text, such as a flower for "lilies of the field," a candle for "let your light so shine," a gavel for "judge not," and so on. He then practiced reciting the text using just his icon list.

Sixth, he envisioned Jesus delivering the Sermon on the Mount, with props that may have been available to him—lilies, birds, the meek and poor, and so on. John noted that as he went through this step, he would ask himself, "What is being taught here?" He found as a result of this that he was able to see more clearly the logical flow of the sermon and story line. He was able to see how concepts like judging and forgiveness tied together, and the whole thing began to make more sense to him.

Seventh, he delivered the lines vocally to himself and then with live props, which were similar to his icons. For example, as he went through the sermon, at appropriate times he picked a flower, touched a thistle, held up a beam to his eye, and pointed to birds in the sky. He also incorporated different body movements to go along with the words. He noted the importance of giving appropriate emphasis, inflections, and expression when stating his lines, and giving the same emphasis or inflection each time he rehearsed. These inflections added audible and consistent variety to the text, which made it easier to remember, especially for a person with an auditory preference.

One other thing John did to improve his delivery and make it more memorable was to videotape his presentation. Not only did this help him identify ways to improve, but it also helped to burn a deeper, more memorable audiovisual image into his brain.

Additionally, he stated that he didn't try to tackle this all at once. He took one section at a time—first the Beatitudes, one thought or idea at a time, and usually not more than five verses a day. He also noted that he reached a point in chapter 6 when his brain seemed to "turn to mush," and all the verses became jumbled together.

At that point, rather than trying harder to unscramble it, he simply put it away for three to four weeks. When he came back to it, he found that his subconscious mind had put everything back in order again. He felt his brain just got overloaded and needed some time to regroup.

That's how John did it. And he did an amazing job in his live outdoor performance, I might add.

Now, let's see how many principles and techniques John used that we have covered. How many did you note? I found twelve. You may have identified even more. This is my list:

First, John used all seven basic principles in the A RECORD formula. He read each section paying close *attention*, not only to the words, but also the themes, the concept flow—what was being taught—and his voice fluctuations. He *related*, or associated different elements in the text to various symbols he was familiar with. He e*nvisioned*, or visualized, the key words, the icons, the setting, and Jesus delivering it. He used *concrete* visual aids, like icons, and later real props.

Finally, he found it was very helpful when he was able to see the order or *organization* in Jesus' sermon, and organizing his icons chronologically was of added value. He obviously had many *rehearsal* sessions over time. This "spaced repetition" seems to be one of the real keys to memorization. And not only did he envision and then practice *delivering* this famous sermon, he actually provided several performances, which no doubt deepened his memories even further.

To enhance his mental images, he not only visualized Jesus *interacting* with the various elements in his sermon, but he acted this out himself using available props and people. He used iconic symbols that *he created and drew* himself. He also wrote out the script and involved other senses as well, especially auditory, in the process.

In addition to what I have noted in previous chapters, John organized his material and practiced it using only his icons. He placed props or cues in his environment to prompt or remind him along the way. He also incorporated body movements like pointing to the flowers and birds, as well as voice inflections to go along with the words. And when his brain got overloaded, he simply gave it a rest. Also, although I didn't mention it, John noted he did a lot of praying throughout this process, especially asking for divine help to make this real and memorable for those who would see his performance. And it was!

Now can you think of anything else that may have helped John accomplish this even faster? One thing that comes to my mind is mental or "memory mapping." John may have gotten a faster start had he developed a memory map of the entire sermon, or at least each significant part, right in the beginning, using key words and symbols. Then he might have focused a bit more on visualizing links or concept connections. This may have given him the sense of order or organization in Jesus' sermon that he notes was very helpful but that he didn't actually pick up until months later. But all in all, John did an outstanding job, especially considering that he had to figure this all out on his own. His process provides us with many good lessons and examples of what we can do to memorize more effectively.

Additional Tips and Techniques

An extension of the idea of adding inflection would be to add rhythm, rhyme, or music, much like the rhymes many of us learned to memorize the number of days in each month (Thirty days hath September, April, June and November), the ABCs, or the books of the New Testament. If you have a musical mind, these can be very helpful, as well as entertaining, to develop.

Scripture verses, however, are usually not as easy to put to song because most songs have lyrical or rhyming words, which Bible verses do not usually have. However, any of this type of interaction with the text requires your attention and involvement, which usually makes learning easier and more memorable.

Overcoming Mental Blocks

One of the keys mentioned by Larry, my son-in-law, that helped to improve his memorization was a change in his self-talk and self-concept. As long as he told himself he had a poor memory for lines or lyrics, he did. But when his new insight enabled him to change his self-perception regarding his memory, he found that his ability to recall what he was trying to store improved dramatically and automatically. This illustrates the power of the self-concept.

As hypnotists and others have noted, the truth is that we all have far greater capacity for learning and remembering than we realize. The problem is that most of us, like Larry, have imposed limitations on our memories. In a sense, we have been brainwashed by a few bad experiences into believing that we are far less capable than we truly are. One of the things that hypnotists do is to remove these self-imposed barriers and set their subjects free to achieve more of their true potential.

You usually don't need a hypnotist, however, to achieve this liberation. In fact, some of the studies on this topic suggest that what we say to ourselves and our own voice are often more powerful than what a hypnotist or some other person might instruct us to do. That is why watching our self-talk is so important for good mental health. If we tell ourselves things like, "I won't remember this," "I can't recall that," or "I simply don't have a good memory," we are in fact brainwashing ourselves into believing that self-limiting line of baloney. If any of those phrases sound the least bit familiar to you, then you need to start using more liberating affirmations.

There are actually two parts to making effective affirmations. The first consists of expressing our desires in a positive, affirming manner, as if they had already been achieved. The second is catching ourselves behaving in accordance with these desires. In essence, affirming to ourselves that what we are saying in our affirmations is true. Effective affirmations of the first kind have three qualities:

1. They are stated in the first person—"I am."
2. They are stated in the present rather than future tense, as if they were already true.
3. They are infused with positive emotion or expectation, again, as if this had already been achieved.

It's apparent that the subconscious mind tends to respond in accordance with, and actually perpetuates, what it believes to be true. In this regard, it acts much like a thermostat—keeping us in balance. So whenever our behavior falls outside of the constraints of our self-concept, our subconscious will tend to pull us back in line.

This of course can be useful in maintaining our integrity and helping us to live in accordance with our highest values and within the behavioral boundaries which the Lord has prescribed. That is true and helpful when we believe ourselves to be good and when we genuinely believe in our own divine potential. It becomes dysfunctional, however, when we believe that we are less capable than we truly are. In either case, it appears that our self- concept, based upon our self-talk, will tend to perpetuate what it believes to be true now, not what we wish were true in the future.

Therefore, whenever you make up your affirmations, make them in the first person, and make sure that they are stated as if they were true, or becoming true. Ideally these affirmations should be stated with some positive emotion and conviction.

Now a word about appropriate emotion—and then on to some affirmations. What emotion would you feel if you suddenly found that you had a terrific memory for anything you had ever read and wanted to remember in the scriptures? Would you be happy, glad, excited, enthused, exuberant? Any of these emotions will be helpful as you make your positive affirmations. An attitude of gratitude is perhaps the most important to maintain. Appreciation for what we have and enjoy is not only one of the most important emotions to feel but also a catalyst to other good things. The Doctrine and Covenants suggests that the lord delights in blessing those who are grateful, who acknowledge His hand and the blessings already received in their lives.

So following these principles and simple guidelines, here are some affirmations you may want to consider using to improve your memory. Keep in mind, however, that these are only suggestions. As with the memory-enhancing images, the ones that will likely work best for you are the ones you come up with on your own.

- I have a great memory.
- I find that I am able to remember more of what I read each day.
- I practice the seven habits of highly effective learners.
- I pay close *attention* to things that are important to remember.
- I *relate* new material to things more familiar.
- I vividly visualize or *envision* the things I am learning.
- I create *concrete* images and associations to tie the text to.
- I *organize* the material I read to make it more memorable.
- I can create powerful vivid mental images for later recall.
- I enjoy mapping new information for total recall.
- I remember well the things that I imagine.
- I can clearly visualize the things I hear.
- I periodically *rehearse* the things most important to remember.
- I often *deliver* or share what I've learned with others.
- I repeat these affirmations daily.
- Each day I'm getting better at applying the things I've learned.
- My memory is improving dramatically.

The next step in using positive affirmations is to notice any time you see one of these positive events occurring in your life and affirming that with a statement like, "Yes, indeed this is becoming more and more my reality!" You don't want to wait for the big "aha's" to do this. The secret is to catch yourself doing the small stuff. Catch yourself making clear concrete mental images and say, "Yes! I'm doing it." Whenever you map a chapter, or memorize a verse, praise your achievement and note, "I'm really getting the hang of this, and it's becoming much easier for me."

Whenever you tie text to a memory peg in a creative or memorable manner, affirm your increased abilities. And whenever you remember to affirm your small achievements and progress, praise and affirm yourself for remembering to praise and affirm yourself. You can say, "See, I'm really getting into the habit of these affirmations. And my memory is definitely improving!"

Interestingly enough, this approach to changing our self-concept is reminiscent of an idea that Alma taught the Zoramites. If you go to Alma 32, you will see that this process is much like planting and nourishing the seeds of faith. Indeed, in making affirmations we are exercising faith that our memory is improving. And like planting seeds in a garden, affirmations are planted in the fertile soil of our mind. Then if we water them, by continuing the affirmations and catching ourselves behaving accordingly, and weed out any sprouts of doubt, we will begin to see the fruits of a better memory unfolding before our eyes. This faith will begin to expand and enlarge our memory, and the fruit thereof will be delicious to our taste. Enjoy!

9

PUTTING IT ALL TOGETHER—APPLICATION

This is perhaps the most important chapter in this book. All the other chapters lead to this one. Because, if you can't put all of these principles, methods, and strategies into practice to help you better remember what you need from the New Testament and conference, you'll have wasted your time.

In this chapter I use a lot of personal pronouns because I want to share with you what I do or what I think works well. That doesn't mean, however, that this is what you should do. Some of these activities and formats may not work for you. I'm just trying to give you some ideas, to help jump-start your brain, to apply the principles and methods contained in this book. You hopefully will come up with some better procedures than I have. When you do, I'd like to invite you to share those with others on my website (www.ARECORD4LDS.com). And if we come out with another edition of this book, perhaps we can include your ideas for even better ways to apply these principles. That's part of the plan, as I understand it, to "instruct and edify each other" (D&C 43:8) for our mutual benefit and progress.

Now, to apply these methods to our gospel study, the first thing we need to do is decide what's most important for us to remember so that when we study, we study with a purpose. When we do, we tend to find and retain more. Also, since we don't have all the time in the world and we do have other things to do, we must be selective in our study. In chapter 2 we talked about the importance of first seeking the Spirit to guide us in this process so we are impressed to focus on that which will be of greatest importance to us and others. In addition to relying on the Spirit to guide us, I like to use another selection criteria from the New Testament. As I'm reading through the scriptures or listening to conference, I'm on the lookout for ideas that seem uplifting, or as Paul put it, "profitable for doctrine, for reproof, for correction, for instruction in righteousness" (2 Timothy 3:16). When I filter that through my brain, I think not only of myself and my family's needs but also those I have a stewardship over, families I home teach, and friends of other faiths. Having had many discussions with my friends of other faiths, I have a pretty good understanding of their questions regarding us. So I'm always on the lookout for verses to share which help to validate our beliefs, as well as other verses or stories which seem to be impressed upon my heart.

On this topic, Elder Henry B. Eyring, in a recent CES (Church Education System) fireside for students counseled:

Since what we will need to know is hard to discern, we need the help of heaven to know which of the myriad of things we could study, we would be most wise to learn. It also means that we cannot waste time entertaining ourselves when we have the chance to read or to listen to whatever will help us learn what is true and useful.[1]

Keep in mind this was aimed at full-time students. But his counsel has relevancy for all of us. We all need "the help of heaven" to know which of all the things we could study, we should study.

Once you have decided on a purpose or set some criteria for what you would really like to learn and have invited the Spirit to be your guide, you are ready to apply the methods.

The following seven steps, if you choose to take them, will help you to apply the various strategies for remembering that we have reviewed so far. These should all be familiar to you. I have just put them together into a logical sequence. You wouldn't need all these steps for casual reading, and you don't necessarily need to do these in this order. But if you really want to remember what you read, applying these seven steps will surely help.

1. Do a quick preview of the material you are about to read to get an idea of the main themes. Formulate some questions and develop a framework for further study (see chapter 7).

2. Fix in your mind an anchor location or setting to tie this information to (see chapter 5).

3. As you read, highlight or circle in red the most important words. This will force you to pay closer attention (see chapter 3).

Then after reading a section—that could be a chapter, a page, or just a few verses to begin with—follow these steps:

4. Create a memory map using the key words, main ideas and whatever additional details you would like to remember (see chapter 7).

5. Turn the map over and see how much you can recall from memory.

a. Note any areas missed.

b. State out loud, underline, circle, color, or otherwise highlight any points that you missed.

6. Imagine what you read being acted out, as in a movie (see chapter 5).

a. Start with the setting or location anchor you selected.

b. Envision a peg word to represent the chapter number, and tie this to the first or main element in the chapter or story.

c. Using the various image optimizing strategies, involve

yourself in the story with as many senses as you can employ.

d. If you are a more auditory learner, make a tape (see below).

7. Discuss or share what you've read with someone else or review this yourself at least twice more that day and each day for the next week.

You will note that in this sequence the story or events are visualized after notes have been taken. The advantage to this is that you will then have all the necessary pieces and their relationships down before you get started. Another way of doing this, however, is to develop the scene or story in your head as you read, taking notes as you go. This will also work for talks or sermons.

Illustrating the Sermon on the Mount

Diagramming and memory mapping, as explained in chapter 7, will help you to organize what you read and hear and will create a more visual model that will be easier to review and remember. Yet, as helpful as these can be, I still find the mental story imagery noted in chapter 5 to be the most memorable for me. And these are faster to create. In fact, most of us create mental pictures naturally as we read, especially when we read stories. The only problem is retention. If we do not make these images clear and powerful, if we do not rehearse them soon after and often enough, they are susceptible to fading and distortion. That is where a diagram, memory map, or other notes can be helpful. I find it best to combine the two, but I don't always start with the diagrams or maps as outlined above. Also I find a few pictures can convey more information in less space than just words. I will illustrate.

You will recall that in chapter 5 we discussed the importance of anchoring information by imagining what you read happening in a specific setting. I also explained the link method for remembering the sequence of ideas being taught. This process of envisioning a set location and linking ideas as you go doesn't always work the best for everything, but it does work well for stories and sermons about life and things (as opposed to more abstract or theoretical concepts). I found it very useful, for example, in remembering the order of lessons and counsel Jesus gave in the Sermon on the Mount, as recorded in Matthew chapter 5–7. For chapters 5–6, I created a memory map. But as I went through chapter 7, I decided to just imagine the scenes, actions, and other images mentioned in his sermon. I'd like to review this chapter with you and illustrate some of the ways I applied the principles we've discussed to make this more memorable for me.

Jesus starts out the chapter on the hill I envision with a huge skeleton key in his right hand (which he gives to a friend of mine named Matthew—signifying this is in chapter 7 of the book of Matthew) and a gavel in the other, with the counsel to not judge others—"For with what judgment ye judge, ye shall be judged" (Matthew 7:2). To create a concrete mental image of this concept, I imagine Jesus holding a judge's gavel in his hand as he talks about this. I then imagine him pointing this at and almost touching the eye of one of his disciples kneeling next to him on the hill, who has a small stick poking out of his eye. This reminds me of his question, "Why beholdest thou the mote that is in thy brothers eye, but considerest not the beam that is in thine own eye?" (v 3). From this intro I can then remember the rest of his counsel—to first take the beam out of your own eye so you can then see more clearly to assist others.

I can also see in the same picture that this disciple has a dog chewing on his sandal. This reminds me of Jesus' next admonition: "Give not that which is holy unto the dogs, neither cast ye your pearls before swine" (v. 6). I see a pig next to the dog sniffing an open oyster shell.

No sooner has Jesus made the statement about them trampling these precious items under their feet, and I see a woman jump to her feet, pull out her empty apron pockets, throw her hands in the air, and say, "But I have nothing to give." I then see a closed door in a door frame appear to her right, and Jesus replies, "Ask and it shall be given you; seek, and ye shall find; knock, and it shall be opened unto you" (v. 7).

On the other side of the door, I see a child tug on his father's robe and ask for bread. The father turns to him with a stone in one hand and a fish in the other, and Jesus asks, "Or what man is there of you, whom if his son ask [for] bread, will he give him a stone? Or if he ask [for] a fish, will he give him a serpent? If ye then being evil know how to give good gifts unto your children, how much more shall your Father which is in heaven give good things to them that ask him?" (v. 9–11).

I then see Jesus walk down to the father and exchange the rock for a golden ruler as He states the golden rule. "Whatsoever ye would that men should do to you, do ye even so to them" (v. 12). (Note that the ruler has 12 inches marked off, and this is in verse 12. What a coincidence!) The man then points the ruler to a very narrow "strait" gate just up the hill to the right, with a narrow path leading to it. Jesus advises them to enter in there, for "broad is the way that leadeth to destruction. . . . Because strait is the gate, and narrow is the way, which leadeth unto life, and few there be that find it . . . and go in thereat" (v. 13–14).

I see a man standing alongside the path, dressed in a wooly sheep's skin. In his hand he offers a thistle. Jesus declares, "Beware of false prophets" (wolves in sheep's clothing), and notes, "ye shall know them by their fruits" (v. 16).

Beyond the gate I see a strait path leading to a house on a rock. I know that this represents "doing" the will of the Lord. And I can hear Jesus saying, "Not everyone that sayeth unto me, Lord, Lord, shall enter into the kingdom of heaven, but he that doeth the will of my Father which is in heaven" (v. 21). He then points to the house and goes on to say, "Whosoever heareth these sayings of mine, and doeth them, I will liken him unto a wise man, which built his house upon a rock" (v. 24). Note how each of these elements or symbols in the story are concrete, easy to remember, and arranged in such a manner that each picture is in some way linked to or associated with the next. Also, several of them are either exaggerated, or quite extraordinary, making them easier to imagine.

Now I know enough about the nature of my memory to realize that even though this scene is clear in my mind now, if I get overconfident, if I don't continue to go over and over this, those images may soon fade. Therefore, it would be prudent for me to make some note of what I have imagined for later reference and rehearsal. But rather than writing this up in a memory map, I decided to just take out a sheet of paper and imagine this representing the side of the hill where Jesus was speaking. I then drew a simple figure representing Jesus near the top. In His right hand I drew a large key, in His left a gavel. I then continued to draw other figures I imagined (or rough representations) to remind me of Jesus' various teachings.

As you can see, to the right of Jesus is a man with a mote in his eye, to the right of him a dog, a pig, and an oyster shell. Below him to the left is a woman with her arms in the air and her pockets turned out, and next to her a door, prompting Jesus' counsel to ask, seek, and knock and God will provide. The figure on the other side of the door represents a small child with his hand clutching his father's garment. His father holds in his left hand a stone. Also in the picture are figures representing a fish and a serpent. This reminds me of Jesus' next statement about what men will give, and Heavenly Father's willingness to give good gifts to those who ask.

The man has a ruler in his right hand, reminding me of Jesus' statement that we commonly call the golden rule. Off to the right is a narrow (strait meaning narrow) gate and narrow way. Next to the path is a figure representing a false prophet—a wolf in sheep's clothing. In his hand is a thistle. Above him, sitting on a rock is a house, reminding me of Jesus' metaphor about the "doer" who built his house upon the rock, as opposed to those who were unwilling to do as Jesus asked, who He likened to a man who built his house on the sand, "and great was the fall of it" (v. 27).

One additional method that I find very effective for review is to summarize and then record the most essential elements of the story onto a cassette or CD that I can then play in the car as I'm driving. This is an especially effective strategy if you are more of an auditory learner. The summary of Matthew chapter 7, as noted above, might be sufficient for that purpose, although I think I would want to add a few more of Jesus' actual quotes.

You will note from the paragraphs above that I've condensed, altered, and added a few things to make it easier to read and remember, while preserving key elements. The King James Old Testament, being an old English translation of a much older Hebrew text, is sometimes written with archaic or rather awkward wording. I'm pretty used to it, having been raised with it. However, I also find the footnotes, Bible Dictionary, and Joseph Smith translations helpful in the LDS King James edition. For example, in verse 13, the gate is described as "strait." However, if you look at the footnotes for this verse, you will see that in Greek this could better be translated "narrow," which makes better sense in this context.

This is also noted in *The New Testament for Latter-day Saint Families*[2], which has a wealth of footnotes to help clarify meanings. In addition, I sometimes use the New American Standard version of the Bible to compare wording. Sometimes it is clearer. I may even add information from commentaries, if they are of significant added value in understanding the concepts. I then record each script onto a cassette, which I play for review on the way to and from work.

For Memorization

I also copy the verses I want to memorize to a file called "NT memory quiz for [topic or chapter]." These are basically arranged as described in chapter 4 under the rehearsal principle and in chapter 6 under remembering names. See the example on the next page. (You will note that this page is set up in "landscape" format. The columns are made using the "Table" tools [in Microsoft Word]). That way, when you add text in one column, it won't move the text in the other columns. (If you set up your columns using "Format—columns," when you enter text in the first column, text in the other columns will move, causing you to have to go back and make time-wasting adjustments.)

You will note that this has been set up to go into my day planner, so I can place them at appropriate times for review, or in a section of their own, where I can just review them when I have a few extra minutes. I can also remove it and put it in my inside coat pocket or tote pocket when I don't carry my planner. Or I can use it as a bookmark when studying the scriptures offline. That way I can easily add additional scriptures or notes while I'm studying.

outside	inside left	inside right
Concept, lesson, or quote: Judge not.	Judge not, that ye be not judged. For with what judgment ye judge, ye shall be judged: and with what measure ye mete, it shall be measured to you again (Matthew 7:1–2).	I see two judges in black robes judging each other. Right after the first judges the second, the second judges the first. I see them using the same scale and measuring cup, and getting back what they give.
Ask, seek, and knock and opportunities shall be opened.	Ask, and it shall be given you; seek, and ye shall find; knock, and it shall be opened unto you: For every one that asketh receiveth; and he that seeketh findeth; and to him that knocketh it shall be opened (Matthew 7:7–8).	I see a woman at a door. First she asks if she can come in. Then she begins to look (seek) for a note left outside the door, which she finds. She then knocks and the door is opened.
Not enough to just call on Jesus to be saved. We must do His will.	Not everyone that saith unto me Lord, Lord, shall enter into heaven but he that doeth the will of my Father which is in heaven (Matthew 7:27).	I see Pharisees in their robes before the gates of heaven, calling, “Lord, Lord,” but the gates do not open. Then a man in work clothes (doer) approaches and the gates swing wide.

I generally try to memorize the King James verses word for word, but at times I modify verses slightly to make them easier to understand and remember. Yet I'm careful to try to retain the original meaning. In translations these are sometimes obscured.

Of course what you use for clues or reminders is up to you. The important thing is that it makes sense to you and effectively reminds you of the verses to be remembered.

This is just one method that I have adopted, because I usually carry my day planner with me. You may want to put your verses to be memorized onto 3 by 5 cards, with the concept or lesson on one side and the verse with cues or clues on the other. I like to use these in the summertime or at other times when I don't have my planner because they can easily fit into any pocket.

This system, you can see, incorporates a variety of principles, learning modalities and techniques to make these sacred teachings more memorable for me.

Common Questions

Now you might think, "Wow! That's really involved. That would take a lot of time." Yes, it does take some time, usually fifteen to thirty minutes to prepare and write up my paragraphs—less for just a few verses, more when I'm doing a recording, depending, of course, on the length and importance of the story, sermon, or chapter. That's why I am selective. I don't do this with all chapters, only the chapters and verses that seem most important for me. On the other hand, that time and involvement is one of the keys that unlocks this wisdom for my life.

Another common question is, instead of taking the extra time it takes to come up with extraordinary associations, memory maps, number peg pictures, etc., wouldn't it be better to just use that time for rehearsal?

The answer is no. There has been a significant amount of research done on this, and while it does take some extra time to apply these learning and enhanced storage strategies, the outcomes in improved retention more than compensate for the extra effort. All other things being equal, information that is vividly stored, especially in sensory rich detail or utilizing extraordinary associations, is typically remembered much faster, easier, and longer than information not stored in this manner.

Like training wheels on a bike, these strategies can help to get our memories started, moving down effective memory tracks, and thus enable us to retain information much faster than repetition alone. Once vivid associations or relationships are formed, it requires fewer repetitions to deeply impress this material into long-term memory for easy future access. Perhaps this is why even those with outstanding natural memories use these techniques. Moreover, their habitual use of these and similar strategies is likely one reason they have such good memories.

Doctors, like attorneys, are required to have good memories, but again their abilities are not without effort. You may recall in chapter 5, I mentioned that while on a book signing in Mesa, Arizona, I met a doctor who for several years taught a course at his medical school to assist other doctors in learning and retaining their studies. He noted that those who took the time to learn and practice various memory strategies and techniques, such as those noted in this book, consistently did better on their exams than those who did not utilize such strategies.

How important is it to have a grasp of that iron rod at all times? Is it worth dedicating this much of your time and talents? As Jesus said, "For what doth it profit a man if he gain the whole world, but lose his own soul [or that of a child]? For what shall he give in exchange for his soul?" (Mark 8:37). I typed that sentence from memory (and it has a few minor errors, but you get the message). Is it not worth some time and effort to have this kind of eternal wisdom ready at a moment's notice, on the stage of your mind, and the tip of your tongue, to help you and yours avoid the rising mists of darkness?

Additionally, I have found these personal scripts, tapes, maps, and quizzes to be a good investment of my time. Sure, it takes some time up front. But now that my tapes and maps are made, it's much easier and faster for me to review this. Plus I can now review these during otherwise wasted time, like driving or standing in lines. I remember much more now of what's important to me in the scriptures than I would if I were to just read for thirty minutes each day. Moreover, since I can't read while I'm driving, I see this as a good, productive, even efficient, use of my time.

On this issue Elder Eyring observed:

> It takes neither modern technology nor much money to seize the opportunity to learn in the moments we now waste. You could just have a book and paper and pencil with you. That will be enough. But you need determination to capture the leisure moments you now waste.[3]

Actually, if you apply what you've learned in this book, you won't even need a book and paper in order to review, reinforce, and apply what you have learned.

Teach the Children—But When?

"And these words, which I command thee this day, shall be in thine heart: And thou shalt teach them diligently unto thy children, and shalt talk of them when thou sittest in thine house, and when thou walkest by the way, and when thou liest down, and when thou risest up" (Deuteronomy 6:6–7).

Perhaps the biggest benefit of this investment of time is that I now have this information available to me whenever I need it. I found, for example, that two of the best times to teach children are not just during Family Home Evenings or family scripture study time but during dinner and while riding in the car. Dinnertime is when my family of origin used to discuss things. Because we lived on a farm, my mother used to say, "You're so darn busy running around doing other things that this is the only time we have to sit down together." I'm not sure that was a good excuse, but dinnertime is a great time to share. I've been gratified to see drug prevention ads recently advocating this time together as a key to drug prevention.

The reason it works, of course, is that once kids get their mouths full, their ears are still open to learn. And they're not likely to get up and leave until they are done eating. Plus some studies suggest people can sometimes relax and discuss better if they already have something setting their jaws in motion—really. Anyway, dinnertime is usually a good time to share the lessons of life.

However, it's awkward to have to run and get your Bible and try to look up scriptures while you are eating. It's better if you have the information memorized and can just tell the stories or quote or paraphrase the most important ideas.

The other good time to share with your children is while you are driving the kids somewhere in the car. For three years, our family lived in England, and during that time our chapel was about twenty miles away. Our children were teenagers at the time, and so we usually made the trip at least a couple times a week for church and Mutual. My wife and I found that was the best time to talk with our children. While riding along, we could find out how school and other things in their lives were going and discuss Sunday School lessons as well as other gospel questions. If they didn't like the discussion (though we usually tried to keep it light), they couldn't just get up and leave at sixty miles an hour.

But again, you can't really pull out your Bible while driving down the road, although your children may be able to if they have them with. You really need to know what the scriptures say. If you can't quote or adequately paraphrase the ones you need at that moment, at least it's good to have your mental pegs in place so you will know where to refer them for the answers and wisdom they need.

Additional Ideas for Young Children

In the next chapter, we go into more depth on how to help others learn. But for now I want to share with you just a few preliminary ideas for helping young children develop a love for and an understanding of the scriptures.

As we all should know, one of the best things you can do for preschool-aged children is to read to them, especially at night before they go to sleep. And of course, some of the best stories to read to them are Bible stories. I can still remember the Bible storybook my mother used to read to me as I sat in her lap in the old rocking chair.

When my kids were small, we would read Bible stories to them as well. As they got a bit older and we got busier, we purchased a set of dramatized Bible stories from Living Scriptures. My son especially loved them. Each night he would play a different tape, until he had heard them all. And then he would start over. He got to the point where he could quote some of the tapes verbatim, before he was five. (Albeit, the scriptures according to Orson Scott Card, who developed the dramatization.) His junior Sunday school teachers were amazed at how much he knew about these Biblical characters. One summer when he was a bit older, we sent him to the local Vacation Bible School with Christian children of other denominations. Again his teachers were impressed at how much this little Mormon boy knew about the Bible, especially when some of them didn't even think we used the Bible.

I believe one of the best things you can do for your children is to help them have some good experiences with the scriptures, to enable them to receive praise and other positive reinforcement at a young age for their knowledge of gospel stories. That can go a long way in helping a child develop a love for the scriptures, as well as a desire to continue to study and remember them and hopefully apply those teachings in their lives.

"I Have a Question" or Totally Useful Teachings—The Game

Some years ago when the Totally Useless Trivia games became popular, I rebelled and got an idea. I asked myself and others, "Why doesn't someone come up with a game that uses totally useful information so families can reap some positive benefits from it, instead of wasting their time on useless stuff?"

In 1998 I started developing such a game. While I never finished all the rules or sold it, I do think it has some positive possibilities. At least I use it and have found it both fun and memory enhancing. It's a great scripture rehearsal technique, either for an individual or group, with many practical applications, especially for parents. Let me share it with you. Perhaps you would like to play it with your family for fun and profit—mentally and spiritually.

In this game we identify scriptures that answer important questions, usually questions having to do with how to deal with life's problems but also questions for missionaries that investigators or friends of other faiths might ask. For our purposes here, these are questions that can be answered with New Testament scriptures. Good questions can be easily developed after finding any good "profitable" scripture. All one has to do is ask himself: What real life question could this story or verse help answer?

Preferably, all who play are familiar with these stories or verses. Ideally, they are also familiar with the principles and methods in this book and have used them to help remember these various New Testament scriptures, and have in fact contributed questions and answers to the game. This makes it a great family game. (At least if the questions are familiar and all family members have contributed some, they will have a definite advantage in the game.)

The game is played by dividing up into teams. One person from each team pulls a question and states: "I have a question." They read the question, and then the other team has to give an answer, preferably using one or more scriptures that address that question. You get one point for a good answer; two if you can answer with a specific scripture, giving the gist of that scripture (at least three words from the verse) and the book it's in or its author; three if you can cite the chapter the scripture is in; four if you can cite more than one scripture that answers the question; and five if you can quote a relevant verse missing three or fewer words per verse. Of course, you can change any of these if the players agree. The point is, the more you know, the more points you get.

Ideally, questions will be divided into groups so there will be questions on various topics. Mine include parenting, interactions with others, handling personal challenges, avoiding temptations, making good decisions, and missionary questions. I've included ten of my favorite questions on the following page to help you get started. I have posted additional questions on my website: www.ARECORD4LDS.com. I invite you to share with me and others some of your best questions and answers via this website.

The other nice thing about this game is you don't need others to play it. That just adds an extra element of fun and gives you a chance to show off your knowledge. But I also enjoy just playing it on my own. When playing on your own, you are, of course, competing against your past performance to see how much more you can remember. But whether it's played on one's own or in a group, it's a great way to learn to apply the scriptures and a super method for rehearsal and scripture memory mastery. Sometimes we learn better as we hear others try to remember information we are seeing. That's the "study helper" phenomena. As you may have witnessed, often the person assisting in test preparation learns the material better than the test taker.

If you are interested in using this method for testing and improving your knowledge of the New Testament, here are a few questions and associated scriptures you may want to use to get started. I strongly suggest, however, that you begin developing some questions and answers on your own. It's fun! Try it. You'll like it! And I can almost guarantee you will be pleased with the strides you make in your understanding and application of the New Testament.

What should we first consider before criticizing another family member?	Our own "beams"—imperfections (Matthew 7:3–4)
When we face the storms of life, what attitude does Jesus suggest we take?	Be of good cheer, not afraid (Matthew 8:24–26; 14:27; John 16:33)
What should we do if another member has offended us?	Go tell them, alone or in private (Matthew 18:15; Luke 17:3).
What scriptures suggest baptism is essential?	Matthew 3:15; John 3:5; Acts 2:38
What must we do after baptism to receive mercy and be forgiven of our sins?	Repent and forgive others (Acts 3:19; Matthew 6:14–15; 18:35; James 2:13).
How should we respond when others say or do mean, hateful, or hurtful things to us?	Do good to and pray for them (Matthew 5:44). Forgive them (Matthew 6:14).
What scriptures show the Father and Jesus are two separate men?	John 8:17–18; Acts 7:55–56; Hebrews 1:3–4
What scriptures suggest God will help you in dealing with tempting or difficult situations?	1 Corinthians 10:13; 2 Peter 2:9
What would the Lord like us to do before taking the sacrament or going to the temple?	Resolve any issue with another person (Matthew 5:23–24).
What scripture(s) from Paul suggest that apostles and prophets are still needed in the church?	Ephesians 4:11–14; 1 Corinthians 12: 28, 18–21
What scriptures give us insight into the unity of the Godhead (how they are one)?	John 17:21–22
Where does it show that the gift of the Holy Ghost was given by the laying on of hands?	Acts 8:17–18; 19:6

In Conclusion

I want to end this chapter with President Heber J. Grant's most famous quote: "That which we persist in doing becomes easier to do; not that the nature of the thing has changed, but that our power to do has increased."[4]

The more you practice these study and memory strategies, the more powerful your memory will become, and the easier and more enjoyable it will be for you to remember what you want, when you want, to share as needed.

Go to www.Arecord4LDS.com for additional insights on applications and game questions.

Notes

1. Elder Henry B. Eyring, CES *Fireside for Young Adults*, May 6, 2001.
2. Thomas R. Valletta, ed. *The New Testament for Latter-day Saint Families* (Salt Lake City: Bookcraft, 1998).
3. Elder Eyring, Ibid.
4. Heber J. Grant, *Gospel Standards*, ed. G. Homer Durham (Salt Lake City: *Improvement Era*, 1941), 355.

10

TEACHING AS JESUS TAUGHT

by Brett Benson

There is one thing needful (Luke 10:38–42), as Christ taught Martha. Jesus came to deliver that message, the most important knowledge the world would ever receive—even His Atonement and the one true path leading to eternal life and exaltation. Christ not only taught the greatest lessons ever given, but He did so by employing the greatest methods ever used. We see, for example, that before He tried to teach the people He first took the time to get their attention and open their hearts to hear. We see this with the woman at the well, the rich young ruler, the chief publican Zacchaeus, Nicodemus, and other desiring disciples. Then He taught them that one thing that each of them needed.

To teach as Jesus taught, a teacher must learn, as the Master demonstrated, the crucial priority of first obtaining the key to the hearer's heart. Many teachers have expressed frustration in their inability to penetrate the minds and win the hearts of their students, especially when they knew they held the needed message. Even the Prophet Joseph lamented: "There has been a great difficulty in getting anything into the heads of this generation. It has been like splitting hemlock knots with a corn-dodger for a wedge, and a pumpkin for a beetle."[1] So what can a teacher do to open the mind and unlock the heart so that a student will listen and pay attention? This chapter was written with that question in mind, first and foremost, of how to prepare even the hardest of hearts so that a teaching may then be received. We will then look at some of the teaching methods and principles Jesus employed.

How to unlock a heart became a subject of serious study when, as a teacher, I had a very hard student that I just couldn't seem to reach. I remembered the principles as demonstrated by the Master, but even then I couldn't seem to do as He did. I didn't know how to reach this student's heart with the kind of love Jesus seemed so able to share. Then a thought came to me: "Even if I can't convey the quality of love the Savior shared, I can at least notice something about this student." I tried it. This was the only way of showing love that I could come up with at the time for this particular student, who seemed to be in an entirely different world. I found I could at least notice her colorful socks, a unique piece of jewelry, or a different hairstyle. That was the level of love I was able to demonstrate at the time. At first there was no change. But then she began to respond. She started to lighten up when she came to class, wanting to be noticed. This attention opened her heart to small talk. Now I could laugh with her and find common ground with her. Eventually I noticed she was listening more closely to what I was saying during the lessons. One day she raised her hand and commented. Before my mouth could drop in surprise, I found myself validating her comment. Soon we were communicating naturally, with her scriptures open and her participation in the lessons increased. At last my hopes for her participation had come to fruition.

And thus we come to the Christ-like preparation that precedes any good teaching. Neil Postman, a famous educator, explained:

> In spite of our attempts to make teaching into a science, in spite of our attempts to invent teacher-proof materials, and even in spite of our attempt to create 'relevant new curricula' one simple fact makes all of this ambition quite unnecessary. It is a follows: When a student perceives a teacher to be an authentic, warm, and loving person, the student learns. When the student does not perceive the teacher as such a person, the student does not learn. . . . Our failure to place affection and empathy at the center of the education process says something very grave about us, and I do not think it will be of much value for us to persevere unless we can learn to love our [methods] less and ourselves and students more."[2]

The greatest thing a spiritual teacher teaches is, after all, the love our Father offered in sending His Son. How can we teach about such love if we don't teach it through love? How can those we teach fully understand the Father's love if they don't feel it from the deliverer of that message? Revelation is something that must be manifest to the mind and to the heart. But in any teacher-student or parent-child relationship, love holds the key, which is turned through the Spirit that opens the heart to such a message in a preparatory way. The key in doing so, as the scriptures tell us, is "by love unfeigned" (D&C 121:41). We can't fake our attempts to emulate the Master. We give only as we truly have. This key comes in knowing that we have each been given a portion of that Christ-like love to share with others, and then finding how best to show that to each individual we seek to teach.

The Prophet Joseph Smith found this same answer for those to whom he earlier had expressed frustration: "Sectarian priests cry out concerning me, and ask, 'Why is it this babbler gains so many followers, and retains them?' I answer, 'It is because I possess the principle of love. All I can offer the world is a good heart and a good hand.'"[3] George A. Smith proved this point about Joseph, telling how the prophet influenced him:

> Joseph wrapped his arms around me, and squeezed me to his bosom and said, "George A., I love you as I do my own life." I felt so affected, I could hardly speak, but replied, "I hope, Brother Joseph, that my whole life and actions will ever prove my feelings, and the depth of my affection towards you."[4]

We must start with what we can offer, giving simply that which comes from a good heart (a smile or a kind word), or a good hand (a handshake, an act of service, or the help that is needed).

Who can therefore best teach the ways of the Lord? He who loves the best. (Love is used as a verb here, for if that love, caring, and concern is not adequately expressed, and received as such, it will likely not be felt by the intended recipient.) But with such preparation, a powerful teaching situation is established. Jesus often exemplified this principle as He established first His love and then His lessons. Through this approach the heart would be open and then the Spirit would be received, not forced. Moreover He directed His disciples to do the same. According to John, before Jesus ordained His apostles to declare His gospel, He revealed this key to opening hearts: "This is my commandment, That ye love one another, as I have loved you. Greater love hath no man than this, that a man lay down his life for his friends" (John 15:12–13).

One day I decided that I needed to teach my son to show greater respect for me. I did so by telling him all of the ways he wasn't. That fell apart in less than thirty seconds. It didn't take long for me to realize I needed to try something different. Instead of demanding respect, I would try winning it with kindness.

Instead of lecturing, I would try to teach it by example—to first show respect for him and his interests. I took some time to find out about his interests. I then did those things with him. We climbed cliffs, we laughed, and we experienced danger. In short, I loved my son into a better relationship. Then, in time, as we traveled and toiled together, great teaching moments came. We were then able to laugh and learn together. We learned that once this condition of mutual respect and love is established, "he that preacheth and he that receiveth, understand one another, and both are edified and rejoice together. And that which doth not edify is not of God, and is darkness" (D&C 50:22–23).

However clever our methodology, it is bound to fail if we fail to first love our learners. Or as the old cliché goes, "People don't care how much you know, until they know how much you care." We must therefore learn to first identify their needs and interests, laugh with them, work beside them, and be patient with them, "reproving betimes with sharpness, [but only] when moved upon by the Holy Ghost; and then showing forth afterwards an increase of love toward him whom thou hast reproved, lest he esteem thee to be his enemy" (D&C 121:43). This concept isn't new. It comes through the example of the Son of God. That's what He did. The Creator descended from His throne above and became a carpenter by trade. He gained understanding and empathy by working side by side with those He would later teach and save. He struggled with them. He obtained water from their same wells. He walked the same dusty paths. He slept under the same skies. Then once he truly understood them, Jesus taught with love. Having done so, He could thus reveal the methods of the true teacher and leader:

"No power or influence can or ought to be maintained by virtue of the priesthood, only by persuasion, by long-suffering, by gentleness and meekness, and by love unfeigned; By kindness, and pure knowledge, which shall greatly enlarge the soul without hypocrisy, and without guile" (D&C 121:41–42).

Such becomes the ideal delivery system of divine teachings to facilitate powerful and effective learning. This is the given way. It is the way of the Son of God. Elder Boyd K. Packer tells the story of a man who traveled many miles to ask a mission president how to spell a word that he needed to place on a form. "Why did you come all the way here?" asked the president. "There are many people who could have helped you with the spelling. You could have gone to the trading post or stopped at the service station."

The man replied, "You are my friend, so I came here."[5] The man could have obtained knowledge from other sources, but he chose to be taught by his friend, and so it is with most people. We are most easily taught and influenced by our friends, those whom we know care about us.

This is also in line with the golden rule and the principle of reciprocity—the most validated principle in all of the social sciences—which suggests that people tend to treat others as others treat them. If we would like others to respect us, we should first show respect for them. If we want others to pay closer attention to us, it's wise to pay closer attention to them. If we want others to listen to us, it's wise to listen to them.

Instead of coercing a student into learning, a wise teacher will first open the mind and the heart of the student by showing genuine love and interest in them, and then wait for the student to come seeking. Isn't this according to the Lord's pattern for teaching? He provides the love, offers the plan, and then waits for the prodigal to come asking, seeking, and knocking. Then that which is needful can be given. What if we did likewise? What if we first demonstrated a greater love for and interest in our students, and then respectfully presented the plan, telling of the eternal rewards that awaited them, and then we patiently awaited the willing seeker? We wouldn't have to coerce, or be frustrated, or lose our cool when the learner didn't react in immediate readiness. We would simply offer, try to persuade, and direct aright, then await the seeking heart.

This leads to the true point of all of this. There is another reason we must deliver gospel messages in the above noted way. Elder David A. Bednar taught of this message:

> When a man speaketh by the power of the Holy Ghost the power of the Holy Ghost carrieth [the message] unto the hearts of the children of men" (2 Nephi 33:1). Please notice how the power of the Spirit carries the message *unto* but not necessarily *into* the heart. A teacher can explain, demonstrate, persuade, and testify, and do so with great spiritual power and effectiveness. Ultimately, however, the content of a message and the witness of the Holy Ghost penetrate into the heart only, if a receiver allows them to enter."[6]

Thus without the background of love, there will be no receiving heart, even with a perfect message. "Readiness is a condition of the heart as well as the mind."[7] We learn this from our Savior, who endured great pain and sacrifice out of His love for us. Now having so established His love, He can teach us all things, and we who have felt of His love, listen. For indeed "we love him, because he first loved us" (1 John 4:19). Likewise, we desire to learn from Him, because we know He wants what's best for us.

Now, having prepared the way through love, Jesus, as the perfect teacher, also employed the greatest methods ever used to teach. These we will review below.

The Teaching Methods of Jesus

We have seen that one of the most powerful methods Jesus used in teaching the multitudes was to teach by example, and He prepared their hearts to hear, as He does ours, through His manifestations of love and service. After first showing a genuine interest in their needs and concerns, after healing them of all manner of afflictions, it was only natural that they would then flock to Him with a desire to hear His words and counsel. But then once He had their *attention*, what other methods did He use to help them to understand and remember his words? Did He apply the other learning principles from the ARECORD formula, noted in chapter 4? Let's take a look.

If we examine the parables and other teaching of Jesus, we can see that, in accordance with the *relate* and *concrete* principles, Jesus often related or "likened" His teachings or more abstract concepts to concrete things that His listeners were familiar with. These included various animals, birds, reptiles, implements, rocks, trees, flowers, a house, pearls, bread, water, wine, and so forth. These were all things they could not only relate to, but easily *envision*. Moreover, by linking his counsel to these common elements in their everyday environment, He not only helped them relate to His teachings but also implanted in their minds automatic reminders. For every time thereafter, that they might see such an animal, object, or plant, they would then be reminded of the teaching associated with this object, animal or item.

For example, many of those He taught were shepherds. If they were not shepherds, it's likely their ancestors had been. These people were familiar with sheep and shepherding. Therefore, Jesus used this metaphor often to describe Himself and His disciples, declaring, "I am the good shepherd, and know my sheep and am known of mine" (John 10:14). To teach the appropriateness of helping others on the Sabbath, He asked, "What man shall there be among you, that shall have one sheep, and if it fall into a pit on the Sabbath day, will he not lay hold on it and lift it out? How much then is a man better than a sheep?" (Matthew 12:11–12)

Something else familiar and loathsome in this rocky land was snakes. It's understandable then that Jesus would compare some unsavory or dangerous individuals in their society with these, as in referring to the wicked as a "generation of vipers" (Matthew 12:34). On the other hand, since snakes were known for being cautious, He encouraged His disciples to be "wise as serpents, and harmless as doves" (Matthew 10:16), doves being a common symbol in their culture for peace.

A few of the other familiar concrete comparisons, or metaphors that Jesus employed, included likening the following:

- Himself to a hen: "How often would I have gathered thy children together, even as a hen gathereth her chickens under *her* wings, and ye would not" (Matthew 23:37).

- The kingdom to a mustard seed (Matthew 13:31) and pearl of great price (Matthew 13:46)
- His work to a yoke (Matthew 11:30)
- Different types of people to different types of trees, and their behavior or the result of their actions to fruit (Matthew 7:16–20)
- Their minds to various types or qualities of soil (Matthew 13:3–9)
- His teachings and foundation principles to a rock (Matthew 7:24)
- Himself to a chief cornerstone (Mark 12:10; Ephesians 2:20)
- Those who complied with His counsel to wise home builders (Matthew 7:24)
- Adversity to rain, wind, and floods (Matthew 7:27)
- Spiritual insight to living water (John 7:38–39)
- The calling of unlearned men to pouring new wine into new bottles (Matthew 9:17)

Next let's consider the organization principle. In the gospel, things need to be presented in order, "line upon line, precept upon precept" as the Lord said through Isaiah (28:10). We can see this same order in Christ's teachings. He and His prophets did not start out by teaching the mysteries of the kingdom. Instead they started by declaring the importance of repentance. You will remember that was John the Baptist's primary message preceding the coming of Christ. In the Sermon on the Mount in Matthew 5, we see a progression from reassuring the poor in spirit to teaching about proper conduct and then striving for perfection. When He sent out his disciples to teach the world, Christ did not tell them to start with a description of the celestial kingdom. No, they were sent to teach the fundamental—first, faith in the Lord Jesus Christ, repentance, obedience, baptism, and the gift of the Holy Ghost, and then other teachings as required (Matthew 28:19–20; Acts 2:38). Similarly Paul told the Corinthians, "I have fed you with milk, and not with meat: for hitherto ye were not able *to bear it,* neither yet now are ye able" (1 Corinthians 3:2; see also Hebrews 5:12–14). It's apparent, therefore, that Jesus did teach, follow, and advocate an orderly or organized progression in gospel knowledge acquisition.

What about repetition or rehearsal? Indeed this too was built into the very structure of the New Testament. Not only did Jesus reiterate the same themes of repentance and obedience over and over, but here we have four different narrators retelling His history and thus reinforcing the images, events, and teachings of Jesus again and again in our minds. But that was not all. In these latter days, the Lord has sent additional witnesses to testify, clarify, and reaffirm His teachings. Not only do we have the New Testament, but we also have the Book of Mormon—Another Testament of Jesus Christ, as well as the Doctrine and Covenants, which again rehearses His most important teachings.

Let's take the concept of dealing with offenses, for example. To some this may seem like a trivial doctrine, but apparently the Lord felt it central to His gospel message because the scriptures contain at least four descriptions of how to deal with offenses. Of course, interpersonal relations—how we are to treat our neighbors—is a central theme in Christ's teachings. And anyone who has been on a mission, or in leadership positions in the Church, or a home or visiting teacher, knows why. Offenses are one of the primary causes of members dropping out and becoming less active in the Church. Jesus not only warned His disciples to avoid these (see Matthew 5:29, 30; 13:41; 18:6) but provided repeated instructions in three of the four standard works on how to deal with them when they do occur (see Matthew 5:23–25; 6:14–15;18:15–17; 3 Nephi 12:23–25 and D&C 42:88–92; 64:8–9).

Then, of course, we have the sacrament which He implemented and instructed His disciples to repeat or rehearse weekly in remembrance of His body and blood which was shed for them. So yes, obviously the Lord understands well the importance of periodic rehearsal or repetition to facilitate memory. He has applied this principle in the scriptures in various ways to help us to remember Him and His most important teachings.

Finally, once Jesus had delivered His sermons and lessons, He directed His disciples to not only apply them but to go out and share or *deliver* them to others (see Matthew 28:19). While it is unlikely that His primary motive was improving their memories for these teachings, no doubt it helped. To share what they had heard would have required them to first recall and then rehearse, and so better reinforce, their recollection of His words.

I would not say that Jesus "followed" the A RECORD formula as He taught the people. Yet in delivering His sermons and parables, it is apparent that He employed these principles, or at least His teachings exemplify the qualities advocated in the formula. In review, He was able to capture His listeners' attention and relate or link His concepts to concrete, easily envisioned things they were already very familiar with. His teachings were organized in a way that made them easier to comprehend. He repeated key concepts often and then commanded His disciples to go out and deliver or share these teachings with others, thus reinforcing the learning within themselves.

Applying the Formula in Our Own Teaching

As we strive to be good teachers at church, in our homes, or in other settings, we would be wise to employ these principles as well. Our teaching will likely be more effective if we can first find a way to capture the attention of our audience and then relate the message we wish to convey to something familiar to and readily available in the environment of our listeners. I am reminded of a stake president who, in an effort to help his youth understand the concept of restoration, likened the church that Christ established in the meridian of time to a grocery store, full of lots of good things to nourish the saints of God. The youth may not have been able to relate to Christ's time period, but they could relate to a grocery store. Then the stake president noted that after

Jesus' departure and the death of His disciples, the store became run down. Much of the food spoiled, and finally the management had to close down the store altogether. But then, through Joseph Smith, this same store was once again established upon the earth—or in other words, we had a reSTOREation, wherein Christ's original store was restored to its original condition.

Of course it likely took this great teacher and church leader a bit of time to develop this meaningful metaphor, but it was something the kids could relate to. More than two years later, some who had been in attendance noted they had never forgotten that comparison. Why? Because the example was not only easy to relate to, it was also concrete, easy to envision, meaningful, and (we would have to say) at least a bit unusual.

I remember a woman in a communication class who wanted to get through to her husband, an avid fisherman, that she had certain needs, which she felt were being ignored. She related her needs for resources, companionship, and personal time for renewal, to his needs for tackle, bait, buddies, peace, and quiet. These were things that were familiar and important to him, and the comparison then helped him to better relate to his wife.

When we take time to follow Jesus' example and relate the concepts we wish to convey to something our intended audience already understands, our listeners are much more likely to pay attention, envision, and remember it. Plus, we will have given them an intrinsic reminder, so every time they encounter that familiar object—grocery store, fishing pole, etc.—or event, they will be reminded of our message.

Helping Children

In helping our children to better understand and remember the scriptures, we can invite them to liken or relate these stories to situations in their own lives that may be in some way similar. This can be done by simply asking them, "Can you relate this to your life? How is this like people or situations you know about?" Have you ever experienced something like this?

Let's say you had a child who was generally a good child, who liked to learn about Jesus but at times was prone to name calling or putting down siblings or others. You might want to share with him Jesus' teachings from the Sermon on the Mount wherein He counseled, "Whosoever shall say to his brother, Raca, shall be in danger of the council: but whosoever shall say, Thou fool, shall be in danger of hell fire." You could note that Raca was a "put down" and then ask, "What do kids say to each other these days that might be like that?" You could also ask if he understands what revile means, and if not, explain the concept. Then ask, "Do kids your age sometimes revile each other? How?"

In the New Testament, particularly the teachings of Jesus, there are many metaphors—concrete words or symbols used to represent other concepts. It is important that children learn how to interpret these or "liken" these to those things they represent. For example, Jesus and other writers often used fruit as a metaphor: By their fruits ye shall know them (see Matthew 7:16, 20). In the parable of the sower, those who hear the word and understand it "beareth fruit" (Matthew 13:23). To help ensure that older children understand the meaning of these metaphors, it is helpful to ask them, "What do you think this means: 'by their fruits ye shall know them'?" What are our fruits? While concrete objects or metaphors are easier to remember, as we talked about in chapter 4, if children do not understand their meaning or what these represent, it will be difficult to apply them in their lives.

Additional Tactics for Teachers

In this section we would like to share with you ten additional methods and messages used by the Savior and other great teachers to facilitate learning.

Teaching through Participation: A certain teacher once told of a very challenging student in his gospel doctrine class. The student came to class every day with a scowl on his face and a defensive attitude toward the doctrines being taught. This wise teacher decided to include this student by inviting him to demonstrate the principles he was teaching. This simple plan changed everything as the student suddenly felt he was on the teacher's team. The defensiveness stopped. He became a leader of the class, helping the teacher to get his points across. This is truly a participatory church and gospel, where each is given an opportunity to get involved, from the war in heaven to missionary work and other church callings. The Lord knows that in the process of doing we come to know. Therefore, He invites each of us, as He did His disciples in ancient times, to participate with Him in His work. It may be wise for us to do the same. Here are some ideas:

1. Invite those who are disengaged to be the volunteers to demonstrate object lessons, the panel that answers questions, the readers, the class presidents, or whatever gives them a responsibility.
2. Involve others in the lesson. Do activities that require group participation—skits, discussions, questions, searches, and so forth. Try to ensure in any group work activity that there is a role for everyone (discussion leader, scribe, presenter, time keeper) and that the activity ends with some kind of class accountability (a report).
3. Give anyone unwilling to engage in any public activity a clerical role such as the birthday list or obtaining things from the office.

Teaching by Example: This comes in two ways. First, some of the most impressive teaching comes from the sharing of personal examples or illustrations of the point being taught. Second, of course, our related conduct can either reinforce or void a lesson. A teacher can't teach what he or she doesn't live. There is no credibility in hypocrisy. Like Jesus, the most effective teaching is accomplished when our actions are in accordance with our instruction. Here are some ideas:

1. Let personal stories add the stamp of living reality to what you are teaching. We could say, "I remember how I felt when I was baptized," or "One day when someone said

something sarcastic to me I decided to . . . "

2. Give examples from their own age group who have lived the principle.
3. Whenever possible remind the students of what the Savior did in similar circumstance, or any modern prophet past or present.
4. Make a special effort to put into practice and allow your students, especially your children, to see your application of the principles you have taught them.

Learning through Doing: Faith follows obedience. In Gethsemane, Jesus prayed, "Not my will but thine be done" (Luke 22:42). In all things He did the will of His Father. What might happen if we taught our students to do likewise? His promise is sure: "If any man shall do my will they shall know of the doctrine" (John 7:17). Here are some ideas:

1. Give them something to do that allows them to practice the principle being taught for a day or a week.
2. Encourage children to practice obedience to parents, and see what results.
3. Encourage adults to practice greater obedience to some principle of the gospel.
4. Have them report what they learned by doing.

One student reported that when his mother asked him to do the dishes, he shocked her by not only saying yes but going immediately to the task. The Spirit then validated his obedience. He later told his classmates what a great change this made in his relationship with his mom for the rest of that day. Not only was he taught, but others became instant "hearers of the word" through the actions of their peer.

Teaching by the Spirit: On the day of Pentecost, as Peter and the apostles testified of Christ, the Spirit touched the hearts of their listeners, and they cried out, "Men and brethren what shall we do?" (Acts 2:37). If we take the time to seek and obtain this same Spirit (see chapter 2) to guide us in our teaching, our students' lives will be touched and they too will feel motivated to learn and live as the Lord directs. Here are some ideas:

1. The testimony of Jesus comes by the Spirit. As we testify of Him, the Spirit enters in.
2. The Spirit will come most powerfully when students accept and live a true principle. Challenging students to commit and do, as noted above, will bring the Spirit.
3. The words of the scriptures were written under the inspiration of the Spirit. Reading them can bring the Spirit into their hearts.
4. The words of modern prophets can be confirmed in the same manner.
5. A student will experience the Spirit more powerfully when bearing his own testimony than when hearing someone else's.

Lead them to the source of truth. Even Jesus did not teach His disciples to glorify Himself, but His Father in heaven. Accordingly, even though we may use personal examples, our objective is not to lead them to us but to Christ and His Father—the true source of wisdom and knowledge. Here are some ideas:

1. Teach of Christ, as a representative of His Father, and of their wisdom, love, and mercy. Consider the words of this song: "Tell me the stories of Jesus I love to hear, things I would ask Him to tell me, if He were here" ("Tell Me the Stories of Jesus," *Children's Songbook*, 57). Help them come to know Him by sharing scenes and stories from His life here on earth.
2. Remind them how much they are loved and to whom they can turn. Ask them, "Do you know how much Heavenly Father loves you? Do you know where you can turn in times of trouble or concern?"
3. Testify of Jesus, His ways, His truths, and His righteousness. Encourage your students to ask and answer the question, "What must I do to come unto Him today?"

Teach the students their responsibility in learning. Like the faithful centurion, real learning will happen only as the students ask, seek, and knock. We must remind them of this admonition from Jesus that they might find out for themselves. Here are some ideas:

1. Teach through the examples of those who have before asked and found such as Joseph Smith, the centurion, Peter, Andrew, Nephi, and Enos.
2. Teach through the examples of those who didn't such as the Pharisees, Laman, and Lemuel.
3. Tell of your own seeking and finding. The Lord gives to those who seek. The promises are great, for if they seek they shall find.

Teach reliance upon the Savior. Jesus taught this in a ship that was sinking. We can do the same, especially when personal ships are faltering in the storms of temptation. Here are some ideas:

1. Point out to students the symbolism in scripture which points to the need for reliance upon the Savior—the rod of iron, the true vine, the rock of our Redeemer, the Way, the Good Shepherd. The list goes on and on.
2. Teach faith in the Lord Jesus Christ.
3. Teach repentance.
4. Teach about the gift of the Holy Ghost and how to discern his whispering.

Help them to see and avoid the tactics of Satan. Like the Savior who came to rescue the captured soul at Gadara, we also play the role of the faithful friend when we come to rescue our students from the grasp of Satan. Here are some ideas:

1. Teach of the traps of the adversary.
2. Warn students of the dangerous worldly trends of the day.
3. Teach of the tactics of Satan.

4. Simply teach the doctrine as it is given in the standard works, and you have just become the most faithful friend that your student could ever have.

Seize Teaching Moments: We must capitalize on the moment. We must remember we are teaching students, not lessons. I once heard a student say to a teacher, "Please tell us the story of . . . " That student was ready to be taught. The teacher answered, "Tomorrow." That should never be our response to that type of request. When students or children say, "I have a question," they have just signaled their readiness to learn. Let's take that moment and teach. They have just opened their heart to hear. Additional events in life allow for teaching moments, such as death, sickness, bad choices and the suffering that follows, fear that follows failure to prepare, a situation at school that is being talked about, and so on. Why wait until the moment is passed? Now is the day of salvation. The time to prepare to meet God is today. Why wait until tomorrow?

An Unforgettable and Concluding Lesson: When Jesus appeared after His death to His chosen Twelve, He had a special lesson for the doubting Thomas. The lesson was that He indeed was real, that His promises were true, that He had the power to keep them, and that men would be blessed for relying in faith on Him.

This lesson remains today. Jesus is the answer to our problems. His is the only way to God. If there is anything that our teaching must do, it is to help us all to remember, seek, and follow Him.

Notes

1. L. Dahl and D. Cannon, *The Teachings of Joseph Smith,* 653.
2. Neil Postman, *Media Ecology Review.* NYU School of Education. Quoted in Brett Benson's Readiness *Techniques that enhance the learning process,* University of Phoenix (Masters Thesis), March 2004.
3. L. Dahl and D. Cannon, *The Teachings of Joseph Smith,* 405.
4. Ibid.
5. Elder Boyd K. Packer, *Teach Ye Diligently.*
6. Elder David A. Bednar, *Seek Learning By Faith.* Address to CES Religion Educators, February 3, 2006. Church Educational System.
7. *Teaching the Gospel: A Handbook for CES Teachers and Leaders* (Salt Lake City: The Church of Jesus Christ of Latter-day Saints, 1994), 13.

11

FOOD FOR THOUGHT

This chapter contains information regarding food supplements and activities that may facilitate memory. However, I am not a doctor, and the ideas, information, and suggestions contained in this chapter are not a substitute for medical attention. Everyone's body is different. What works for one person may not be good for you (see examples below). If any significant adverse changes occur in your health or memory, we suggest you see your physician. Additionally, if you are on any type of medication, especially coumadin or other blood thinners, or if you are under a doctor's care for any reason, check with your doctor before trying any new nutrients or physical activities noted in this chapter.

In chapter 3 we talked about the two different aspects to memory. These I labeled natural memory, composed of organic gray matter, and memory processes. We then discussed a variety of memory processes or procedures and various ways to improve these. Usually, these processes, or the lack thereof, are the weakest links in memory and the easiest to fix. Unfortunately, many people come to believe that they have a poor natural memory (insufficient gray matter when in fact their primary problem is they just don't know how to effectively use what they've got to store what they see and hear). That is why we started with those procedures. Hopefully by now, if you have been implementing the seven habits and associated methods, you have found you have a much better memory, or more capable gray matter, than you had previously supposed. It just needed a bit of training.

On the other hand, a variety of conditions could have a negative impact on our natural ability to remember. These include age-related deterioration in the structures of our brain, oxidation, plaque that can build up in the brain, some prescription medications, poor circulation of vital oxygen and nutrients, and the resulting degeneration in the supply of chemical messengers or neurotransmitters, particularly acetylcholine. Fortunately, it's nice to know we can do many things to prevent or overcome these conditions and improve the quality and capability of our natural memory (gray matter). In this chapter we will talk about some of the foods and nutrients you can take, as well as other things you can do to help support healthy brain functioning and keep your memory sharp and clear.

Again, for a quick review, we noted in chapter 3 that the brain needs the following in order for it to function at its optimal capacity:

1. Healthy cerebral cellular structures
2. Neurotransmitters
3. Good nutrition
4. Plenty of oxygen
5. An effective circulatory system

I indicated:

> All the above noted elements need to be performing their own proper function and working in concert with each other, and not inhibited by any other harmful substances, including drugs or medications. If any one of these five elements is missing or seriously depleted, or if other substances are inhibiting proper brain function, it will usually manifest itself in some type of mental or memory deficit. Even a low-grade problem, in one or more of these areas over time, can result in memory storage or retrieval problems. In short, a person, thus afflicted, simply won't be able to recall what they want to, when they want to, even though they feel they ought to be able to.[1]

You may remember, but it bears repeating, that there are many reasons a person might experience problems with his natural memory physiology, the most common being vascular or circulatory problems. Therefore, it is always best to consult your physician or a neurologist if you are experiencing a significant decline in memory to determine the most likely cause. Otherwise you could end up wasting a lot of time and money pursuing blind alleys when the light, in fact, lies at the end of another path. The nutrients (described in this chapter) and strategies (described in Chapters 4–10) of this book can prove useful in preventing or dealing with a wide variety of memory problems. But the more you know about your specific needs, the better you and your doctor will be able to develop a program that is effective for you.

I noted in chapter 3 that I once went to see a doctor because I was worried about my natural ability to remember. I was referred to a neurologist and then a psychologist, who put me through a battery of tests. The conclusion was that some of my problem may have been stress induced. I had a lot on my plate at the time, and high stress can impair memory, especially over time, and especially when it leads to a lack of confidence in one's memory. But other than that, my natural memory was fine, or at least adequate.

So we discussed procedures that I might follow to improve my recall ability. Actually I found that I knew more about these than the psychologist who was treating me. I just wasn't applying them as I should have. Once I realized this and started applying the seven habits and optimizing strategies, I found that I was able to achieve remarkable memory feats. But I also started taking a variety of food supplements and doing a few other exercises that may have helped as well. Let's now review those other things you can take and do to strengthen your memory.

Helpful Nutrients

It was once thought that the brain was somewhat immune to nutritional deficiencies. We now know that this belief is false. The brain needs more nutrients, including glucose and oxygen, than any other part of the body. When deprivation lasts for too long, problems begin to occur. For example, studies in every decade since the 1960s have found that children who did not eat breakfast were not able to concentrate and do as well in school as children who did.[2] Their gray matter just wasn't getting what it needed to function well. Most healthy adults, who do not have blood sugar problems, are less vulnerable to this fasting phenomena. In fact, most adults suffer more memory problems from eating too much than from eating too little. Large meals draw blood from the brain and can often leave one feeling lethargic and unable to focus. More frequent, smaller meals would likely serve us better. Also, as we advance in years, the body begins to lose some of the enzymes and nutrients needed to break down and assimilate protein and other food that the brain needs to create neurotransmitters and the mechanisms of memory. Therefore, we once again become more vulnerable to malnutrition and memory problems. A study of 260 Albuquerque residents over the age of 65 found that those with the lowest intake of various nutrients consistently scored lower than the rest in memory tests.[3]

The primary food for the brain is glucose. About 25 percent of our daily calories are devoted to brain functions. The body can synthesize glucose out of various foods, but if a person doesn't eat much, his brain may become starved of this most fundamental fuel as well as other necessary nutrients. A study in the *British Journal of Clinical Psychology* reported: "Women on very low-calorie diets displayed poorer reaction speeds, immediate memory and ability to sustain attention, compared with the women who were eating a moderate amount of calories."[4]

Of course it's not just people on diets who are vulnerable to mental malnutrition. Calories and nutrients can lack whenever one loses his appetite, whether it's from high anxiety, stress, stomach upset, or as with some elderly, when they just don't feel like eating. At an elder care center where I once worked, I noticed that often when we began to see a decline in memory or an increase in confusion, it coincided with reduced healthy food intake.

Smart Nutrients

What are the nutrients necessary for memory? Simply put, all of them. That is why it is so important to have a well-balanced diet. Ray Sahelian, M.D., author of *Mind Boosters*, notes our diets should include fruit, vegetables of various colors, grains, nuts, and seeds. He also suggests we vary our fruit and vegetable intake and try new kinds of produce. Some best for the brain include "citrus fruits, berries, apricots, grapes and other fruit. Your vegetable intake should include garlic, onions, green leafy vegetables, yellow- or orange-colored vegetables, tomatoes and beets."[5] These foods, especially in their raw, or unprocessed state (after a thorough cleaning to remove wax and pesticides), and *when taken in sufficient quantities* should have all the vitamins, minerals, enzymes, proteins, and fats that the brain needs to function well. And yes, I said *fat*. Most people do not realize it, but polyunsaturated fats or fatty acids (PUFA) are the primary building blocks of the brain. That's why a mother's milk is so high in fat, particularly DHA.

But, you might ask, "Where's the beef?" Doesn't one need an abundance of meat and dairy products to provide the protein and calcium the body needs? Certainly the brain needs some protein as well as calcium, but probably the best sources of protein for an aging brain are beans, particularly soybeans, nuts, seeds, and sea greens, not meat. While beef, pork, and lamb are good sources of high-quality protein and vitamin B-12, they are also sources of saturated fat. It may seem paradoxical, but while unsaturated vegetable, grain, nut, or seed fats are essential for adult mental health, saturated fats, the kind that turn solid when left to stand at room temperature, can have the opposite effect. Additionally, Dr. Sahelian suggests we "decrease [our] intake of fried foods, margarine and baked goods. These foods contain trans-fatty acids and hydrogenated oils that interfere with the function of good fats."[6] These fats can also slow down mental functioning, and through oxidation may even cause damage to brain cells. They also add unneeded cholesterol to arteries, which tends to raise blood pressure and restrict the flow of other nutrients to the brain.

In one study at the University of Toronto, Carol Greenwood, Ph.D., and her colleagues found that animals fed diets high in polyunsaturated fats learned about 20 percent faster than animals that were fed lard or just regular chow. And they were less likely to forget what they had learned, suggesting improvements in both short- and long-term memory. Red meats are also reportedly harder for the body to break down, and large quantities can divert enough blood from the brain to make one mentally sluggish.

It's no wonder then that when King Nebuchadnezzar offered Daniel and the other three wise Israelites meat and wine, they asked for foods made from seeds, grain, fruits, and vegetables (pulse) instead. As a result, "in all matters of wisdom and understanding" they were found to be "ten times better" than all the other "learned or wise men" in his realm (Daniel 1:20).

Personally, I am not a vegetarian. Having been raised on a farm with cows and pigs and chickens, I enjoy eating all of them, especially fatty bacon. But the above-noted research, as well as other sources, do suggest that Daniel and his friends knew what they were doing when they asked for pulse. Joseph Smith was indeed inspired in writing the Word of Wisdom where we are counseled to eat meat sparingly. Therefore, I seldom eat much beef or pork anymore because I know they can impair my memory. While I still eat most meats once in a while, I realize that some are likely better for me than others.

Fish has long been considered a brain food. Not only is it a good source of protein, but the oil in most fish, especially salmon and other cold water fish, is an unsaturated source of omega-3 fatty acids, including DHA (docosahexanoic). These fatty acids form the essential structural components of brain and retina cell membranes. That's one reason mothers' milk is so high in DHA. Additionally, omega-3 fatty acids assist in breaking down the bad HDL cholesterol in our arteries. They also function as antioxidants and counter inflammation that can damage brain cells. Eating fish has also been linked to improved circulation, so important to healthy brain function and memory.

It's no wonder then that "a study of 815 people age 65 to 94, found that those who consumed fish once or more weekly had 60 percent less risk of developing AD [Alzheimer's Disease] than those who did not."[7]

Other fish high in DHA are halibut, mackerel, sardines, and herring. These fish feed on algae, and most algae is an excellent source of protein, vitamins, and minerals as well as DHA. (It just doesn't taste quite as nice as a freshly baked salmon.) But if you've ever wondered how Nemo and his father were able to find there way home, now you know. However, Dr. Joseph Mercola, author of the Total Health Program, notes that because these fish are prone to absorbing "dangerously high levels" of mercury, dioxin, PCP, and other metals, the risk in eating these regularly or in large quantities may outweigh the benefits. One exception is Alaskan wild red salmon from the Bering Sea. These so far have not been found to contain such toxins. Another, a less risky and easier option is to consume fish oil or omega-3 rich cod liver oil. Dr. Mercola notes, "While I am well-known as a minimalist when it comes to supplements, fish oil (in the warm months) and cod liver oil (in the cool months) are 'supplements' that I strongly urge you to add to your daily diet if you want to prevent disease and increase both the length and quality of your life."[8]

If you do not care for fish or fish oil, there are not many other good plant sources for omega-3 that contain DHA except flax seed oil, and of course blue green algae or purified DHA supplements made from algae. A newer option is DHA-rich eggs laid by chickens fed DHA-supplements.

I have been studying and teaching about nutrition for the past twenty years, and one fact that remains true is that while many nutrients have been isolated and can be purchased in pill form or taken in teaspoons, the ideal way to get these building blocks of life is through whole, unrefined, organic, or nutrient-rich foods. Why? Because in this whole food form, vitamins, minerals, proteins, and lipids have what are called co-factors, trace minerals, enzymes, and other micro-nutrients that help our bodies get the most out of our food. Therefore, it is important to get a good variety of nutritious whole foods, and not to overcook them. Cooking some foods is essential. Yet, on the whole, most of us overcook more than undercook. Most of us eat more processed, refined, or neutered food than fresh fruit or raw vegetables.

For example, which do you eat more of—potato chips or carrot sticks? Carrots are an excellent food full of vitamins and minerals, but potato chips are basically saturated fat and salt, both of which in excessive quantities can contribute to clogged arteries and starved brain cells.

Two other items important for our mental health are water and sleep. Many people don't get enough of either. Dr. Sahelian suggests drinking "one or two large glasses of water when you wake up in the morning to help empty the colon."[9] Of course, it's important to drink water throughout the day as well. Water is one of the most important things we can take to help remove toxins and keep our body and mind working as they should.

Adequate rest is the other essential. The brain needs a good night's sleep in order to process and retain the things we have learned. Students who do not get adequate sleep do not do as well in school. If you are not getting the sleep you need, do what it takes to ensure that you do. It can really make a difference.

Finally, it appears that once a problem has developed, it may take more than a maintenance dose of certain nutrients to get the brain back on track. It is also not surprising, therefore, that some food supplements have proven very helpful in facilitating various cognitive abilities, including memory, both in children and adults. In the next section, we will take a closer look at some of these essential nutrients and evidence of their efficacy for improving memory.

Specific Nutrients for Memory

From a basic building-block perspective, some of the most necessary nutrients for the brain and memory are the "B" vitamins, often referred to as B-complex. These include B-1 (thiamine), B-2 (riboflavin), B-3 (niacin/niacinamide), B-5 (pantothenic acid), B-6 (pyridoxine), B-12 (cobalamin), folic acid, biotin, choline, and inositol.

The B vitamins work in concert with each other to provide a host of services necessary for digestion, assimilation, damage prevention, relaxation, attention, and memory. Scientists have long been aware that deficiencies in the Bs can produce a variety of symptoms associated with memory loss. For example, B-12 and folic acid are necessary to form myelin, the insulating sheath that surrounds the neuron and enables message transmission. B-1 serves to protect this sheath from the damaging effects of alcohol, smoke, and aging. It also enables the brain to utilize carbohydrates for energy production. Deficiencies in B-12 and folic acid are often associated with depression and memory problems, as in the Albuquerque study noted above.

B-1 deficiencies have been shown to result in anxiety, irritability, confusion, aggression, depression, and poor memory.

B-2 is needed to produce anti-stress hormones, and deficiencies have been linked to mental confusion, sluggishness, insomnia, and depression.

B-3 has been shown to improve the memories of middle-aged patients 10 to 40 percent.[10] It also helps prevent anxiety, confusion, paranoia, and depression.

B-5 helps protect neurons and provides support for the adrenal glands, which help the body handle physical and mental stress. Low levels of this nutrient have resulted in increased tendencies to anger, low blood pressure, stomach upset, and physical weakness. It may also play an important role in the synthesis of acetylcholine, which is vital for memory.

B-6 is necessary for the synthesis of other neurotransmitters called catecholamines, which help keep us alert and optimistic, and facilitate learning. Deficiencies in B-6 can also lead to anxiety, depression, and, in some case, seizures.

B-12 deficiencies are commonly associated with dementia, and sublingual (under the tongue) supplementation has been shown to facilitate the learning of new material.

Folic acid aids in the production of several neurotransmitters including acetylcholine and serotonin. Therefore, a deficiency has been found to produce irritability, forgetfulness, mental lethargy, and depression. (Most anti-depressant medications are aimed at increasing serotonin levels.)

Choline provides the raw material for the production of acetylcholine and has accordingly been found helpful for improving memory, especially when taken in conjunction with other B vitamins.

Doctor Jay Lombard, a board certified neurologist, and Carl Germano, a clinical dietician, in their book *The Brain Wellness Plan* state, "We cannot overemphasize the importance of adequate B vitamin intake for a healthy nervous system and proper brain function."[11] They further note the best dietary sources for these nutrients include whole grain bread, cereals, pastas, and meat. They also suggest adding a complete B-vitamin supplement to the diet. The B vitamins seem to work synergistically with each other. To facilitate memory these authors suggest doses of 50 mg per day, taken with or just before meals.

C, E, and Free Radicals

In the previous section, we noted the brain has a great need for oxygen. Although it contains 2 percent of our body weight, it utilizes 20 to 30 percent of the oxygen we consume. Additionally, this gray matter needs a great deal of blood to carry this oxygen, as well as other nutrients, to all the regions of the brain. One of the problems with this system, however, is that with oxygen comes oxidation and free radicals. Oxidation is what causes rusting and an elastic to lose its elasticity when left out in the elements too long. It results in the brown pigment that discolors the uneaten portion of a half-eaten apple. The brown spots that we develop on our bodies as we get older are said to be evidence of this oxidation process going on inside our bodies. Indeed oxidation is a leading cause of aging, including an aging memory.

Free radicals, or reactive oxygen species (ROS), in the biological sense, are tiny, unstable, and incomplete molecules with a single electron. Free radicals are naturally produced during normal metabolism, and some are a necessary part of our immune system. However, like sparks from a fire, they can damage and weaken other tissues and cells they come in contact with by robbing them of their electrons. These reactive oxygen atoms can be very damaging to cell membranes, proteins, enzymes, and even DNA. They are, therefore, considered a primary player in the aging process but more particularly in neurological degeneration because of the high rate of oxygen consumption in the brain.

How to control internal oxidation and free radicals is currently a hot topic of discussion in Alzheimer's research. While researchers don't blame oxidation and free radicals for AD per se, it seems oxidation and free radicals are critical factors in a chain of reactions that eventually result in brain damage, tangled cells, and the loss of vital mental functions.

Various factors can increase the production of free radicals, including stress, exposure to pollutants from autos, pesticides, radiation (UV light), alcohol, and various drugs. Illness, infection, inflammation, and other health problems, including diabetes, arthritis, and asthma, also increase production of these molecules, as does LDL cholesterol and elevated blood sugar. Many stimulants and metabolic enhancers such as caffeine and diet pills also produce free radicals, but so do eating and exercise to some degree.

Our bodies deal with oxidation and free radicals through the use of antioxidants. Antioxidants are powerful little compounds that prevent oxidation and mop up free radicals. They are abundant in various foods, and some are referred to as flavonoids. That is why when you squeeze lemon onto the uneaten portion of an apple, it will not discolor as rapidly. Vitamin C is a potent antioxidant. Perhaps it is because of this greater need for antioxidants that the brain reportedly needs up to fifteen times more vitamin C than the rest of our body.[12] Vitamin C also facilitates the synthesis of acetylcholine and norepinephrine, both of which are vital to memory. It is not surprising, therefore, that numerous studies have shown a direct link between vitamin C and memory. In one study of 351 students, researchers found that while lower levels of vitamin C corresponded with low levels of alertness, increasing plasma levels of vitamin C by 50 percent resulted in a 3.5 percent increase on IQ tests.[13]

Because the body does not manufacture vitamin C, we must rely on dietary sources. Citrus fruit, broccoli, peppers, and other dark-colored vegetables are good sources of vitamin C. (The less acidic and more readily assimilated form is called calcium ascorbate, or palmitate, and is available in health food stores.)

Vitamin E, another powerful antioxidant, has also been shown to facilitate a variety of cognitive functions and even help prevent or slow the progression of Alzheimer's Disease. In his book *Achieving Optimal Memory*, Harvard psychologist Dr. Aaron Nelson reviews two recent studies on Vitamin E. The first, published in the *Archives of Neurology* in 2002, looked at 2,889 individuals, ages sixty-five and older, with normal memory and cognitive function. After tracking this population and their nutritional intake for three years, researchers found that those who consumed the most vitamin E showed 36 percent less mental decline over the course of the study than those who consumed the least.[14]

Another reason vitamin E is able to produce such seemingly miraculous results is because of its positive influence on the vascular system. In other words, it helps to keep our blood system in good repair so that oxygen and other nutrients are able to supply our mind's many needs. In an earlier study involving 3,385 Japanese American men ages seventy-one to ninety-three, researchers found "those who reported taking vitamin C and E supplements had an 88 percent lower incidents of vascular dementia (which is related to stroke) compared with men who didn't take the supplements. The rate of dementia was lowest among men who'd taken the vitamins the longest."[15] The lesson from that study, of course, is, don't delay. If you don't currently take either of these vitamins, you may want to start today. Wheat germ, unsaturated vegetable oils, seeds, and nuts are all sources of vitamin E, but most of us don't get enough from our food, so a wide variety of these supplements are readily available.

CAUTION: Vitamin E can affect blood platelet function and promote bleeding. For those with certain blood disorders, such as hemophelia, high doses can be dangerous. If you are on any blood thinners such as coumadin or anticoagulants, talk with your doctor before increasing your intake.

Ginkgo Biloba

Research in Europe and now in the United States has begun to focus on other compounds that may prove even more powerful than Vitamin E in preventing oxidation, quenching free radicals and improving circulation. Likely the best documented at this time is the herb ginkgo biloba.

In October 1997, the *Journal of the American Medical Association* (JAMA) published an excellent multi-center study using double-blind empirical (scientific) methods that showed conclusively that an extract of ginkgo biloba was in fact effective in helping to alleviate cognitive problems in the early stages of Alzheimer's and other forms of dementia.[16] Although there was little to no improvement in the control group who did not take gingko, at least 40 percent of those in the ginkgo group experienced a *significant improvement* in their thinking and functioning abilities, including memory, and the progress of AD was at least retarded in another 20 percent. Moreover, no significant negative side effects were found from this treatment.

As noted, the primary way in which ginkgo appears to help memory is by facilitating circulation or blood flow to the brain. If memory problems are caused by poor circulation, ginkgo may help, but additionally ginkgo is an antioxidant, free radical scavenger, which appears to help reduce the damaging effects of AD. A more recent study, however, did not find that Ginkgo had much of an effect on healthy individuals. While it may help prevent some degeneration, it may not do much to improve your memory if your organic memory is basically normal.

CAUTION: Because ginkgo may have a tendency to thin the blood, if you are already on coumadin or any other type of blood thinner or anticoagulant, including aspirin, you should consult your doctor before taking ginkgo.

Other Potent Antioxidants

Some months ago I visited with the owner of a health food store who told me about vinpocetin, another plant compound, that may be significantly better than ginkgo for improving circulation to the brain. Vinpocetin is an extract from the periwinkle plant (vinca minor). "It selectively dilates the arteries and capillaries in the head area, which improves circulation to the brain . . . and may help improve memory."[17] It also reportedly helps increase brain cell ATP (adenosine triphosphate—the cellular energy molecule) production as well as the brain's utilization of glucose and oxygen. It apparently performs several functions in combination that are important for the brain and memory. It's no wonder then that more than a dozen empirical (scientific) studies have shown it to be helpful in improving both the speed and accuracy of natural recall abilities.[18]

Vinpocetine is reportedly used extensively in Europe to treat a variety of mental conditions to include cerebral insufficiency, aphasia (loss of the power of expression), and apraxia (inability to coordinate movements) resulting from stroke, dizziness, inner ear problems (including tinnitus), reduced visual acuity, insomnia, and mild depression, in addition to improving memory and learning abilities, with minimal to no side effects.[19]

I believe the moral of this story is, if you are thinking of taking ginkgo to improve your cerebral circulation and memory, you may want to consider vinpocetine instead, since it appears to provide more avenues for possible improvement of natural memory.

The information I've read on vinpocetine notes that while some users feel improvements within the first few days, others may not see major improvement in the above-noted conditions for months (if at all). It is reportedly best to take with food since some nausea has been reported when taken on an empty stomach. And like most supplements, the improvements you see may regress if and when you stop taking it on a regular basis. However, it is generally considered safe for long-term usage and may be worth a try. Vinpocetine is available at most health food stores or can be ordered online.

CAUTION: Like ginkgo, vinpocetin may have a tendency to thin the blood. If you are on coumadin or any other type of blood thinner or anticoagulant, including aspirin, you should consult your doctor before taking Vinpocetin.

Because antioxidants are so important in preserving our internal systems, God has provided an abundance of them, in a variety of sources in our environment. In addition to vitamins C and E, ginkgo, and vinpocetine, some of the most powerful include acetyl-L-carnitine (ALC), alpha lipoic acid, glutathione, n-acetyl-cysteine, selenium, carotenoids, pycnogenol, grape seed or fruit polyphenols, coenzyme Q-10, and tocotrienols. All of these have proven to be potent antioxidants, and most have shown at least some degree of effectiveness in preserving mental faculties, including memory.

Most of these antioxidant free radical scavengers can be found in the foods we eat, or ought to be eating. However, if a person is not eating well and oxidation appears to be taking its toll, all of the above can also be found in supplement form. When taking antioxidant supplements to facilitate memory, you should consult your physician. While few side effects have been found in clinical studies, it is possible to consume too many antioxidants in pill form. Those familiar with this field suggest that it is best to go with a variety at lower doses. It would seem prudent to follow the instructions on the label unless otherwise indicated by a physician familiar with these nutrients and the condition of your body. Most doctors, however, will not be familiar with all of the above nor all that follows. You might encourage them, therefore, to purchase a copy of *The Brain Wellness Plan* by Dr. Lombardo and Carl Germano or *Mind Boosters* by Ray Sahelian, M.D.

Supplements to Increase Memory Messengers

Another of the newer antioxidants to hit the market, which may help to increase acetylcholine and improve memory is huperzine A. This traditional Chinese herbal remedy is prepared from the moss huperzia serrata, which has been used in China for centuries to treat fever and inflammation. Although this particular compound does not appear to reduce fevers or inflammatory, hupA does seem to be a potent inhibitor of acetylcholinesterase (achE). An esterase is an enzyme, which in this case breaks down excess amounts of acetylcholine—the primary chemical messenger for memory.

In addition to helping patients with Alzheimer's,[20] hupA seems to be of significant value for those with less serious memory problems. At present, it appears to be safe, and it is relatively inexpensive, but not enough research has been done to determine long-term safety or side effects. Therefore, Dr. Sahelian recommends its use only for those with AD and only under medical supervision. I have mentioned it here for your future consideration, or in case you know someone with Alzheimer's Disease. Because it is relatively new on the market, you will likely find it available only in health food stores.

If you are over the age of sixty, another nutrient worth considering is phosphatidylserine (PS). If a cell is damaged or in a state of disrepair, it will not be able to perform its required functions. Phosphatidylserine is one of the most essential elements in our brain and is needed not only to protect against free radicals but also to repair and rebuild damaged cell membranes. Additionally, PS is necessary to metabolize brain fuel—glucose. It's no wonder then that studies have shown supplementation with PS to be helpful in restoring healthy mental functioning.[21] The problem is, most of the studies to date were conducted using PS from animal sources, but that is not available to the public. PS derived from soy lecithin is available in health food stores, and Dr. Thomas Cook, who conducted much of the early research on PS, believes it to be nearly as effective.[22] However, more recent research has not proven that. Nevertheless, I do know of several elderly individuals who have found it quite helpful. If you are over sixty and can't seem to remember what you read or hear as well as you used to, you may want to discuss this nutrient with your doctor.

Important Minerals

Antioxidants and lipids may do much to prevent damage to memory cell membranes and mechanisms, but they do not provide the other nutrients that the brain needs to function at an optimal level. The complex of B vitamins may get us off to a good start, but minerals may be just as important.

Calcium and magnesium are two more important minerals essential for healthy functioning. While calcium is an important constituent of the electrical impulses used in nerve communication, magnesium assists in the production of other neurotransmitters, as well as ATP as noted above, a key element in the production, storage, and transference of energy. And remember, the brain uses a lot of energy. Because these two minerals are so important to so many processes, deficiencies are not uncommon in mature adults. Its also important to note that the body needs vitamin D, the sunshine vitamin, in order to make the most of calcium, as well as another trace mineral called boron. In one study of an elderly population with cognitive impairments, many of the residents were found to be deficient in boron.

Other trace minerals such as selenium, copper, and zinc have also been shown to be important for a healthy, effective memory. These three minerals play important roles in the production and function of several neurotransmitters and enzymes related to memory. I take a formula[23] with minerals and trace minerals in it daily, just to be sure, and if I miss a few days, I can tell a difference.

The supplements I have tried and found helpful for me are DHA, vinpocetine, and hupA. I also take grape seed daily as well as a low-potency memory formula,[24] containing the B-complex vitamins, vitamins C and E, choline, L-Tyrosine, gingko biloba, ginseng, gotu kola, green tea extract, and trace minerals. If I feel my head is congested or I have a bit of a cold or headache, which I seldom have, I've also found an aspirin or half an aspirin helps my memory. But a tall glass of water and a good long walk will usually do the same thing for me.

However, there's an important concept to keep in mind here. It's called biological individuality, which basically means that each of us is different. Just because something helps me, that doesn't mean it will do anything for you. So it comes back to what I said in the beginning. If you feel you have a problem with your natural memory ability, it's best to start out by going to see your doctor. Have him or her check out any medications you are on to see if they might be causing this, and then have a thorough check up. It's hard to fix a problem if you don't know what's causing it. And with memory problems there can be many different causes.

Moreover, this approach can save you both time and money and may even save your life.

Once you know what the problem is, you and your doctor can discuss alternatives. That is when you may want to share with him or her some of the information noted above to see if any of these may be useful for you to try. It should be noted that all of these are over-the-counter, unrestricted, food supplements that you should be able to pick up at almost any good health food store and many grocery stores. Moreover, none of the foods I've reviewed here are noted as having significant negative side effects when taken as directed on the label. If you feel your natural memory is not as sharp as it could be, these are some supplements worth considering. At least you may want to take a good look at your diet to see if you are getting enough fruit, vegetables, and omega-3 fatty acids in your diet. But there are other things you can do as well to improve your natural memory that won't cost you a penny.

Mental Exercise

As our baby boomer population continues to age, I'm sure we will find many more things that are important to keep our minds sharp and clear. But we already *know* a great deal more than most of us *do*. Rather than giving you another long list of things to do, I will just suggest a couple of things that have multiple benefits, and then provide a few references for those with deeper interest.

In chapter 2 and then again here, I have talked about the importance of oxygen and good circulation for our body and brain and particularly our memory. Even though your brain typically makes up only 2 percent of your body weight, it takes up to 20 percent of your body's total intake of oxygen. It's also important that we find ways to reduce the stress in our life and relax. In light of that, it should not be a surprise to learn that one of the best things you can do for your body and brain is aerobic exercise. Aerobic exercise does all of those things for us. It increases nutrient assimilation—we get more out of the food we eat—and have better oxygen circulation to the brain. It reduces stress and helps your body to relax afterwards. Physical exercise also stimulates your brain while physical inactivity and watching TV tends to numb it.

Basically, aerobic exercise entails any type of vigorous exercise that causes you to breathe extra hard for at least twenty minutes. Jogging, biking, swimming, hiking, jump rope, or a good, hard game of basketball, handball, racketball, or tennis all qualify. But one of the best is just a brisk, twenty- to forty-minute walk, especially if you have high blood pressure. Brisk walking gets your circulation going, increases oxygen intake, improves digestion, is low-risk for accidents or injury, and is easily accessible and easy on the joints. Furthermore, it seems to help rid our body of adrenalin and cortisol, the stress hormones. As a result, exercise, particularly walking, if done regularly, has a soothing or calming effect on the nervous system, which tends to lower blood pressure.

I've found if I get "writer's cramp," have a problem I'm stumped on, or just need to get some new ideas or words flowing, a good walk, with my pocket recorder, is one of the best things I can do. I personally have found, like many others, that I think much better when I'm walking. I ran cross-country in college and still do some jogging, but I don't often get those runner's highs or endorphin surges. Perhaps I'm too distracted worrying about my knees wearing out. In any event that's not the best time for me to think. Walking really seems to help get my mental juices flowing. It also seems to facilitate information recall. If you want your mind to stay sharp and clear, you may want to seriously consider getting more regular vigorous exercise, at least twenty minutes a day, five times a week, preferably more.

But what if you can't exercise? Perhaps you are confined to a wheelchair or have some other condition that prevents you from walking briskly—like a very tight schedule or pressure-packed meetings in your Sunday suit. Well, then, you still have two options.

There are, of course, other exercises that you can likely do other than walking. I have a friend who is confined to a wheelchair, and he still gets out and puts miles on his wheelchair, albeit a special chair, and gets a good workout. But even if you can't get out of the house or you are confined to a bed, there are other exercises you can do by stretching elastic bands. There are also isotonic exercises in which muscular contractions occur without movement of the involved parts of the body—like clasping your hands and pushing each against the other. You can even do these in long meetings. Any physical therapist could show you a variety of these. These exercises can help get your blood circulating, tone your muscles, and even increase your heart rate and breathing.

In any case, you can always practice the next exercise, and that is deep breathing, one of the benefits of exercise. That alone can help improve circulation and oxygenation of the brain and perhaps even weight loss. Yoga has some interesting breathing exercises. But just sitting up straight or standing against a wall and breathing deeply enough to lift your chest, holding that a second or two, and then exhaling fully, counting to seven and repeating that for even a couple of minutes, will help. Longer may be better (see *Brain Builders* pages 249–253 for more advanced breathing exercises).

If we do not get enough oxygen to our brain, we will simply not be able to think and function as well as if we did. That's the bottom line. So remember to breathe. When reading or working at the computer or on other inside projects, remember not to stay slumped over for too long. Such a position can restrict oxygen intake and may hamper retention. At least every hour, if you are not confined, get up from your desk and go get a drink of water. Most of us don't drink enough water either. The body and mind need movement, oxygen, and H_2O. Within reasonable limits, more is better for our brain.

The final category of exercises are specifically for your mind and memory. Even if you are totally paralyzed physically, or nearly so like the great physicist Stephen Hawking, any type of sensory stimulation and deliberate thinking—reflection, envisioning, imagining, linking, recalling, calculating—according to Richard Leviton, author of *Brain Builders*, "seem to produce an immediate increase in blood flow into the brain."[25] With that in mind, some of the best things you can do to stimulate or exercise your brain and improve your memory are the exercises contained in this book. Developing those extraordinary and vivid images in your mind, linking them (as in developing a strategy for recalling all the books in the New Testament) and recalling the contents of chapters (pegging concepts to chapter numbers, memory mapping, memorizing, playing the "I have a question game") will stimulate your brain and do much to keep your mind and memory sharp and clear well into your later years.

For more information on brain building or memory exercises, you can go to any local library or bookstore and look for books on memory improvement, usually in the psychology or self-improvement sections. Four of my favorites still in print are *Brain Builders* noted above; *Don't Forget*[26] by Danielle Lapp, Ph.D., a professor at Stanford University School of Medicine; Dr. Whitaker's *Boost Your Brain Power* cited earlier; and of course *Your Memory, How it Works and How to Improve It* by Kenneth Higbee, Ph.D, from Brigham Young University.

For more up-to-date information on nutrients and exercises for the brain and memory, go to chapter 11 under Additional Helps at www.ARECORD4LDS.COM/additional_helps/index.htm.

Notes

1. See chapter 3: The Anatomy of a Great Memory.
2. See the Child Nutrition Policy Brief from the Food Research & Action Center, Washington, D.C. (www.frac.org/pdf/cnnl.pdf), for a review of recent studies on this issue.
3. Goodwin, James S., Goodwin, J.M., & Gary, P.J., "Association between nutritional status and cognitive functioning in a healthy elderly population," *JAMA*, June 3, 1983, vol. 249, no. 21, 2919.
4. "The Memory Menu," *American Health*, May 1998, 62.
5. Ray Sahelian, M.D. *Mind Boosters*, 50.
6. Ibid., 49.
7. "Bottom Line Yearbook 2006" (Stamford, CT: Boardroom, Inc., 2005), 92.
8. Dr. Joseph Mercola, www.mercola.com/2004/sep/15/omega3_alzheimers.htm.

9. Ray Sahelian, M.D., ibid., 50

10. Dr. Julian Whitakers, *Boost Your Brain Power*, 91. Also in Richard Leviton's, *Brain Builders: A Lifelong guide to sharper thinking, better memory, and an age proof mind,* 224.

11. Dr. Jay Lombard and Carl Germano, *The Brain Wellness Plan*, 37.

12. Richard Leviton, *Brain Builders*, 214.

13. Dr. Julia Whitaker, ibid., 97.

14. Aaron P. Nelson, Ph.D. & Susan Gilbert, *The Harvard Medical School Guide to Achieving Optimal Memory*, 85.

15. Ibid.

16. LeBars, PL, Katz, MM, Berman, N, Turan, M, Freedman, AM, Schatzberg, AF. "A placebo-controlled, double blind, randomized trial of an extract of ginkgo biloba for dementia," JAMA, Oct 22/29, 1997 vol. 278, 16, 1327.

17. Ley, Beth M., *Marvelous Memory Boosters* (Temecula, CA: BL Publications, 2000), 23.

18. Ibid. See also I. Hindmarch, et al. "Efficacy and tolerance of vinpocetine in ambulant patients suffering from mild to moderate organic psychosyndromes," *International Clinical Psychopharmacology,* 6(1):31–34, Spring 1991.

19. Ibid.

20. Dr. Ray Sahelian, 176–178.

21. Amaducci, L. "Phosphatidylserine in the treatment of Alzheimers disease: results of a multicenter study." Psychopharmacology Bull 1988; 24 (1):130–4. And Amaducci, L., Crook T. H., Lippi A., et al. "Use of phosphatidylserine in Alzheimers disease." Ann NY Acad Sci 1991; 640: 245–9. Both cited in Lombard & Germano, op. cit., 72.

22. Thomas H. Crook III, & B. Adderly *The Memory Cure.*

23. This solution is called Liquid Gold, and is mined from an ancient Utah source rich in trace minerals. This company also carries "Trace Minerals that Taste Good." (They come in a variety of flavors and do actually taste good.) For more info go to www.landofhealth.com or write to: Land of Health, P.O. Box 914, Layton, UT 84041.

24. This formula is called "Memory Magic" from Land of Health. (See 14.) Other nutritional formulas for memory can be found in most health food stores.

25. Richard Leviton, *Brain Builders* (Englewood Cliffs, NJ: Prentice Hall, 1995), 250.

26. Danielle C. Lapp, *Don't Forget* (Cambridge, MA: Perseus Books, 1995).

12

HOW TO MAKE AND BREAK HABITS, AND OTHER APPLICATIONS

Be ye transformed by the renewing of your mind.
—Romans 12:2

This final chapter contains a three-for-one special offer. With one simple technique, I will show you a method for (1) making the seven habits of effective learners an ingrained part of your daily life, (2) ensuring total recall of anything you want to remember in the New Testament, general conference, and beyond, and (3) overcoming any bad habit, including pornography and addictions. Moreover, you will learn how to do all three at the same time! All at no extra charge! And, oh yes, as an added bonus (as if this weren't enough), this technique will also enable you to reduce, if not eliminate, the influence of Satan and his demons in your life.

Some years ago I worked in a center that specialized in helping people overcome bad habits to extend their life. One day, while working with an LDS client, I believe I felt inspired to suggest the following technique. The essence of this technique is reconditioning our brain so that promptings to perpetuate bad habits will cue us to cultivate a new, healthier habit. But before I get into the details of this strategy, let's talk a bit about habits.

Every January for five years, I taught a series of classes on how to keep New Year's resolutions. The class was called "Changing Course." One of the reasons I liked to teach the class was that I knew I needed it. As I noted in chapter 4, teachers learn more from teaching a class than the students who attend. And I always had one or two pesky habits I wanted to overcome. If I ever ran out, all I had to do was suggest to my wife that I felt that I was approaching perfection and *voila,* she instantly made me aware of one or two more issues that needed attention. Anyway, in those sessions, getting down to the nitty-gritty of changing habits, I learned the following:

- Behavioral habits are supported by thinking habits, or associations. Some habits are simply thinking habits such as worrying. Anxiety, fears, phobias, and depression are all a result of related habits of thinking. These thinking ruts can be very deep, self-reinforcing, often hard to self-identify, and, of course, hard to break out of.
- Substitution is a key to breaking bad habits. You can't just focus on stopping a habit. This will only cause you to think about it more. You must come up with a more constructive, incompatible habit or behavior to replace it with.
- Some habits are perpetuated by the adversary, Satan, whose desire and design is to thwart our progress and see us miserable. And He is not to be underestimated. But . . .
- God can and will help us, even in miraculous ways if we seek Him in faith.

Since this is not a book on habit control per se, I'm not going to go into any greater depth on the first two insights. If your habit is one primarily of thought control, such as anxiety or depression, what follows may help. However, I also recommend you read *Feeling Good* by David Burns, M.D. If your condition is serious, regardless of the nature of the habit, you may want to seek professional counsel from a psychologist or psychiatrist familiar with the principles of cognitive behavior theory.

Regarding the third insight, when working on habits that affect people's self-esteem or spirituality, if I could recondition a client to respond to the same perverse promptings with a righteous action instead of the former degrading or self-defeating habit, often those promptings would go away. This makes sense if you believe there are evil forces that can and do entice us to degrading or self-defeating behaviors.[1]

Think about it. If every time you were enticed to do or think something unrighteous or degrading, you instead allowed that temptation to remind you to do something good or uplifting, after a while these demons might see the futility in their attempts and stop their promptings,[2] at least on that matter. And, in fact, I've found in many cases, this is exactly what happens. Or at least it appears so. I can't say for sure whether this is a spiritual phenomenon or merely psychological. All I know is that it usually works or is at least helpful. Moreover, it is in line with how Jesus responded to temptations.

The account of the Savior's response to Satan's temptations, as recorded in Matthew 4, provides an excellent example of how we can overcome temptation.

"And when he had fasted forty days and forty nights, [the Savior] was afterward an hungered. And when the tempter came to him, he said, If thou be the Son of God, command that these stones be made bread." The Savior responded, "It is written, Man shall not live by bread alone, but by every word that proceedeth out of the mouth of God" (Matthew 4:2–4).

Notice that Jesus didn't just respond by citing scripture but rather by citing a scripture about the importance of scripture, thus making the point doubly strong. In fact, Jesus responded to three temptations by citing scripture. This suggests that perhaps the best way to deal with temptation is to fill our minds with the word of God—scripture. If we do not have the word of God treasured up in our memory, we may not be able to properly respond when temptations arise. In other words, we oppose the temptations of passion or the physical "natural man," with their opposite—the spiritual.

Now I will show how this approach can work with one of the major and most challenging plagues of our day—pornography. One of the reasons pornography can be so addicting is because of its chemical bond to memory. Pornographic images can effect the release of norepinephrine, which causes the brain to print the pornographic image deep into memory, making it easy to evoke and hard to get rid of. Pornography can actually stimulate a wide cascade of powerful chemistry, perhaps the most powerful that we have in our bodies because it is tied to essential elements necessary for the perpetuation of life. And as you are likely aware, once it gets going, this combined chemistry can be an extremely powerful, driving force, leaving a person with a deep, almost insatiable thirst for more.

Unlike other appetites, this urge, once triggered, is not easily satisfied and doesn't easily subside. Even then, it doesn't take long to regenerate and begin its drive again, especially in a young, male body. The more we give into it, the more it demands as it drives a person toward reproduction or sins of biblical proportion.

For someone who is married, these passions can be an incredible source of enjoyment, can help draw a couple closer together, and can lead them to the sacred role of becoming co-creators with God. However, if the object of a person's desires is outside the bonds of matrimony, it can only lead to frustration or, worse, condemnation.

If you want to read the lamentations and pondering of a tortured soul who learned this lesson too late, you only have to read 2 Samuel 12:1–12 and the sad Psalms of David, particularly Psalms

6:6, 38:1–11 17–18, and 88. No wonder David's son Solomon gave such stern warnings on the subject (see Proverbs 5:1–14; 6:24–35; and chapter 7).

So how can the seven habits help? Recall that the first of the seven principles of memory, reviewed in chapter 4, is *attention*. We remember most and best those things to which we pay close attention. Unfortunately, in our environment there are many inviting cues (reminders, triggers, hooks) to catch a man's attention and make him vulnerable to further promptings from the adversary to pursue more of those images.

As noted, people who are addicted to pornography often experience very strong urges and promptings to pursue this addiction, to seek more and more explicit images, and in time perhaps to view even perverted images. One of the best methods to overcoming this habit is to avoid paying attention to it in the first place. In other words, we should avoid media (magazines, R-rated movies, salacious TV programs, and so on) that portray these provocative, eye-catching images. For women, this might not be movies or magazines as much as romance novels or daytime TV, which evoke mental images of licentious scenes. Obviously, the more we can avoid these in the first place, the less we'll need to deal with the consequences.

However, total avoidance is almost impossible in our society, especially when you walk through a mall and see ten-foot high window dressings or, more accurately, un-dressings; pass through a multitude of men and women who wear provocative clothing; and see obscene magazine covers in checkout stands and lascivious ads on TV and the Internet. The triggers are everywhere and nearly impossible to avoid all the time. However, do you remember what we said when describing short-term memory and the attention principle? Just because something is in our field of vision, we don't necessarily remember it unless we focus on it and pay attention to it for more than a second or two.

Also remember the displacement principle. If, after seeing an image, we can shift our focus to something different for more than a minute or two, that initial unwanted image will soon fade and be replaced by something else. Now we are getting closer to the method I want to share.

Sometimes we are caught off-guard. Maybe we're pulled into a conversation or we inadvertently glimpse an image, and before we know it, we are feeling an enticement to pursue—to look longer or ponder something that we know we should not. What can we do when this happens? The key is in prior preparation. If you wait until you are in the midst of enticement to try to decide what to do, it may be too late—or at least harder. In other words, the sooner we turn away, the easier it will be. The key is pre-decision.

By pre-decision, I mean before we get into that situation, we decide exactly what we will do. Dr. Richard Novacco developed this approach for dealing with provocations to anger.[3] He called it anger inoculation. First, he would discuss with his clients the typical things that provoked them. Then he discussed appropriate alternative responses and had them decide on one or two that they felt would work for them. Next he invited his clients to get into a relaxed, comfortable position and have them picture themselves in a situation where someone would say or do something that would normally provoke them to anger. Once they could imagine this provocation, he asked them to take a few deep breaths, relax, and then imagine themselves making an appropriate response. Dr. Novacco had his clients practice this over and over with various provocations and responses. Thus, they learned to recondition their response pattern. A previously provocative comment or action would now evoke a much more measured and appropriate response.

The same method can be applied to almost any bad habit or undesirable response pattern, from biting your fingernails to drug addictions, from thoughts of worry and anxiety to depressing thoughts. Our feelings and behaviors are almost always a result of our dominant thoughts and focus. If you choose to control your thoughts (and we all can with a little practice) and what you pay attention to, you can control, to a major extent, your feelings and your subsequent behaviors. The key is to choose appropriate familiar thoughts and replacement responses ahead of time. Then make sure you use the replacement response when the cues or triggers are encountered.

This is in line with 1 Corinthians 10:13: "God is faithful, who will not suffer you to be tempted above that ye are able; but will with the temptation also make a way to escape." We can always choose to focus on other things. And it will make that choice much easier, in the time of trial, if we have chosen good alternatives beforehand to shift our attention to.

Every Sunday we are promised in the sacrament prayers that if we will always remember the Savior, we can always have His Spirit to be with us. How could anyone who loves the Lord commit a sin, if at the same time they are remembering Him? It's highly unlikely. I believe that remembering Him includes those things that He has taught in the scriptures. Are they not virtuous, praiseworthy, uplifting, and of good report? Indeed, as Paul noted, They "are able to make [one] wise unto salvation" (2 Timothy 3:15).

Steps for Mental Reconditioning

It's difficult, if not impossible, to simply stop a bad habit like smoking. The more a person tries by willpower alone to stop smoking, the more he will likely think about it. And the more he thinks about smoking, the more he will want to smoke.

The real secret is substitution. You've got to come up with and focus on implementing another incompatible habit in place of the habit you wish to change. Someone trying to stop smoking would be wise to focus on developing better habits of exercise, perhaps deep breathing when tense, drinking more water and grapefruit juice, or eating more sunflower seeds. Then when thoughts of having a cigarette come to mind, these individuals use that as a reminder to think about how they are doing or what more they could do on those other habits. Or perhaps the words of some song that they like will help, or some scripture like, "I can do all things through Christ which strengtheneth me" (Philippians 4:13). Any mind-consuming mental exercise, like recalling and reciting relevant scriptures, as Jesus did, will help.

Again one of the best strategies for overcoming any temptation and developing good habits is to recondition that temptation so when it comes, it reminds us to review and do something good. Since temptations and enticements are everywhere, or at least are now frequently getting your attention, they provide a perfect reminder to practice what you have learned. If used in this way, the enticements of Satan can actually help remind you to develop a better memory for the wisdom and truths taught in scriptures, or in other words, to get a better grasp on the iron rod.

Ironically, the primary reason readers do not apply the methods mentioned in this book is that they forget. Not being in the habit of studying in this fashion, most of us will simply slip back into our old read-and-forget mode. However, by using the substitution method, we can make our bad habits and temptations serve us by prompting us to practice and implement these new habits of memory.

Clearly, the real key to distracting us from bad habits is to focus on something else that requires our *full attention* and the active use of our mental faculties. Therefore, reviewing or memorizing scriptures, or recalling lessons from the scriptures, is an ideal substitution. This is one of the most demanding mental tasks that we can undertake, next to creating those images, so they can be effectively stored in the first place.

Another reason for learning and remembering verses from the scriptures is that these can provide wisdom that will help us deal more effectively with any daily challenges in life. As we're told in the Doctrine and Covenants, if we will "treasure up in [our] minds continually the words of life, it shall be given [us] in the very hour that portion" needed at that moment to deal with whatever temptation or problem may come our way (D&C 84:85). Pondering the scriptures will also bring the Spirit into our minds and hearts, which can further facilitate that process.

The following are a few of the many mental exercises or

habits you can develop to shift your attention off things that are not uplifting and focus it on that which is praiseworthy. If an undesirable thought comes to mind, do the following:

- Try to recall what you last read in your daily scripture study.
- Try to recall scriptures you have previously memorized that increase your faith, courage, and moral strength.
- Review in your mind the main points of a recent conference talk.
- Practice reciting all the books of the New Testament in order.
- Recall to mind a memory map of a chapter or talk that you have constructed, in as much detail as possible.
- Think of a challenge a family member is facing. Then review scriptures you can remember and identify one that might be of help in this situation. If you have applied the method for remembering the location of scriptures, try to recall from memory where each of those scriptures is located.
- Think of someone else who could use encouragement, perhaps someone you home teach or visit teach, and try to think of a story or verse from the New Testament that might help or encourage them.
- Carry around scripture cards of verses you want to memorize and peg to their location. Pull one out and work on memorizing it or developing a memory cue to help you remember its location in the future.

The Lord told Joseph Smith to "let virtue garnish thy thoughts unceasingly; then shall thy confidence wax strong in the presence of God" (D&C 121:45). These are all virtuous lines of thought that can keep your mind from wandering into the paths frustration, sin, and sorrow, while at the same time help increase your confidence and lift both yourself and others.

Confidence, or what the scriptures call faith, is critical. It can be helpful to remember that we are children of God with great divine potential. And furthermore, we have been given a special gift, even a member of the Godhead, to comfort and guide us, if we see and receive Him. As you remember to apply these principles, you must affirm your progress, as we noted in chapter 8. As you do so, you will feel a further increase in confidence and self-esteem, which will help to propel you on to victory and greater self-control.

In review then, here's how you can use the principles and methods you have learned for improving your memory to help you overcome any bad habit or temptation and to turn the enticements of the world to serve you in improving your memory for the scriptures:

1. First, identify the bad habit or temptation you wish to overcome.

2. Jot down those things that prompt you to think about or engage in that habit. Note thoughts and images you may encounter or that may come to mind, including things that others say or do that get you going in a destructive, depressing, or wrong path.

3. Note mental tasks (like those above) or habits that you are trying to learn or develop. Ideally they will involve the scriptures. It's a good idea to write these tasks, or new habits, on a 3 by 5 card to carry with you. In times of crisis, the faintest ink can be better than a flustered memory.

4. Find a time and place where you will not be interrupted. Get into a comfortable position, sitting or lying down. Then imagine being presented with one of those temptations. See yourself responding by shifting your focus to the memory task you are trying to develop. Take out the card if you need a reminder. Then in your mind rehearse the verses, talk, or association you are trying to learn.

5. Practice this over and over at least daily for the first week. Each temptation and your more appropriate response or new habit pattern should be imagined at least three times. Then move on in subsequent sessions to imagining other temptations or provocations, replaced each time by the response habit or memory task

you are trying to develop. At the end of every session, it's important that you see yourself successfully overcoming the bad habit and developing the new one. Then imagine how much better you'll feel about yourself when you have developed that response habit or memory task.

6. Next, practice this in live situations. Again, you may want to use your 3 by 5 card to prompt you initially, but in time the new memory response will become what is called a "conditioned response or habit."

7. Finally, reinforce any positive progress you make. Tell yourself after every session, and particularly every time you respond appropriately to a real temptation, "I can do this! In fact, I just did! I'm getting better, and it's getting easier all the time." Then let your mind ponder the rewards that will come as you continue this behavior.

CAUTION: Satan is no dummy. Never underestimate his power or cunning. King David did, and he paid for it for the rest of his life. Satan will try to draw you back into your old habits in any way he can. Keep up and vary your practice. Then, "pray always, that you may come off conqueror; yea, that you may conquer Satan, and that you may escape the hands of the servants of Satan that do uphold his work" (D&C 10:5).

If Satan gets the best of you on occasion and drags you back into your undesirable behavior, repent. Learn from the experience and get back on track. Self-recrimination, calling yourself names, and beating yourself up are usually counterproductive and can become disempowering tools of the devil. They tend to reduce our self-concept and make us even more vulnerable. Don't let Satan discourage you. Keep your eye on the end result. Note the lessons learned in your notebook for future review so you can grow from your temporary slip up, and then move on with the program.

Remembering to Remember

What if you are one of those rare souls who doesn't have any bad habits to replace? How can you develop other positive reminders to help you get into the habit of remembering your scriptures? How can you remind yourself to remember and trust in Christ so that you might always have His Spirit to be with you to direct and guide you?

If you don't have enough outside influences providing cues for you, develop some on your own. And it's not hard. Remember, all that your memory needs is a hint, a small cue or trigger to get it going in the right direction. Of course, you could make up big signs to post in prominent places that read: "Remember to rehearse and apply your scriptures." Or: "Remember Christ."

That could work, and may be the most effective. However, other simpler, more versatile methods are also available. One of my favorites is dots. Buy or make colored dots that you can stick to things. Make a mental note that whenever you see one of these dots, you will think of Christ and review a scripture in your mind. Be sure to place the dots in places where you will see them during the day, such as on your bathroom mirror, your rearview mirror, the refrigerator door, or the screen of your computer.

If you do choose to use the dot system, don't ignore the dots. This too could become a habit, and then they will be of no value to you. It's better to respond to the dots as soon as you see them for at least three weeks. Respond to a dot by rehearsing a scripture when you first see it; then continue on with what you were doing. It's kind of like doing your home teaching by the first week of the month. You feel good that you've done it.

Once you've developed the habit, you can take the dot down or start developing a different habit with a different color. You will find that as you begin treasuring up on a regular basis the words of eternal life, it will be easier to remember them, and Him, and "it shall be given you in the very hour that portion that" you will need (D&C 84:85).

Remembering to Do Our Duties

In the first chapter, I noted that sometimes we get so caught up in things, even good things, that we *forget* to do more important things—like keeping our commitments to others, fulfilling church assignments, and attending the temple. I know it can be frustrating to give assignments and count on people to show up, and then they don't. Of course, I have been the one who didn't show up at times! Maybe it's my experience with the latter, as well as my awareness of the fragile nature of memory, but I have come to the conclusion that when "active" members do not show up for assignments or events, it's not that they are rebellious, so much as they simply forgot. The simple fix? We need more tangible and appropriately placed reminders, cues we can't help but pay attention to.

Many of us simply assume that otherwise responsible people will remember these things. But without a reminder, and with so many other things going on in our lives, we don't. At work I use a day planner for all my appointments. However, I don't take that to church with me. In some callings, I had another binder, but I didn't always remember to review that when I should have during the week. So now I make notes on the back of our church bulletin and then transfer those notes after church onto our family calendar. This hangs near the telephone where we can easily review it throughout the week. Whatever method you use, it's important to develop a single method of reminders and use that one method consistently until it becomes a habit. And if you want to make sure others remember their assignments or appointments later in the week, do what your dentist does—call them. That will increase attendance by at least 50 percent.

Now, I could develop a memory system for keeping track of these assignments and events in my head. However, for such transient tasks, I prefer the adage, "The shortest pencil is better than the longest memory." But one must also get into the habit of reviewing those hen scratches regularly.

Other common challenges are remembering our commitments to family members during the day or week. And akin to this is reminding ourselves of things we need to do during the day, especially when we don't have a pencil on hand, or we think of something while driving the car.

Several memory tricks can assist with this sort of task. One of the simplest and most effective is tying a string on your finger. A variation of that is changing your watch from one wrist to the other; then, the next time you look for the time, you are reminded of whatever you associated with that change. I usually carry a comb, pen, and 3 by 5 card. If I think of something while driving, I hang the pen or comb from the front of my shirt. Then when I stop, I'm reminded and can write notes down. I sometimes also carry a small pocket recorder to record important thoughts and ideas.

If you have no method to write or record a task, you can use your memory and local cues to prompt you. For instance, imagine you are driving in your car when you remember that you need to call Mary to set up a time to plan Saturday's party. You also need to bake a cake for tonight and clip coupons for this afternoon's shopping. So you come up with a picture that contains all of those activities, and then you mentally tie it to something you will soon see in your house—like the door going into the house from the garage, the mudroom, stairs, or entryway.

For example, let's imagine entering your house from the garage. On the steps leading from the garage to your house, you imagine Mary, and she looks a wreck (to make it more memorable). It looks like she just stuck her face in a cake because her face is covered with frosting. She also has a pair of scissors hanging from her hair. Imagine this scene vividly. You might even imagine touching the frosting and licking your fingers to involve more senses. Then if your mind wanders to other things, as it usually does, when you arrive home and start walking up those stairs, that image will flood back into your mind and you'll remember to call Mary, make a cake, and clip those coupons. With practice, these memory reminders can be fun and have many different applications.

In Conclusion

I hope the strategies I have shared in this book have been encouraging and helpful for you. I hope your mind has become energized with the possibilities for enhancing your capabilities to remember the scriptures as well as the many other benefits that can accrue to you and your loved ones as a result of these increased abilities for retention and recall.

One observation: While these methods and ideas have proven effective, if you do not apply them, you will lose them, as well as all the knowledge you could have retained had you persisted in applying them. I speak from experience. As I've noted, I have used these methods off and on throughout my adult life. Being able to retain in remembrance a knowledge of the scriptures has been a great blessing to me and my family. I hope it is now a great blessing to you. But too often, I've felt I was just too busy to take the time to work up more vivid pictures or a few memorable links or pegs for better retention and retrieval.

As I've worked on this book, I've been haunted by thoughts of what might have been if I had just taken a bit more time to apply these principles and methods more consistently in my life. What if I'd done just a little bit more every day and every week, worked up my game plan earlier, and been more persistent in my study and rehearsals? I'm saddened to think how much better prepared I would be.

Think what a great wealth of wisdom you could have readily available to bless the lives of others, if you will just persist in applying these principles. Do not procrastinate your application of these lessons. We are talking about the word of the Lord, the iron rod, words of salvation, great wisdom and eternal life, of which, wise Solomon said, "All the things that may be desired are not to be compared to it" (Proverbs 8:11).

In Matthew 6, the Lord says:

> Lay not up for yourselves treasures upon earth, where moth and rust doth corrupt, and where thieves break through and steal: But lay up for yourselves treasures in heaven, where neither moth nor rust doth corrupt, and where thieves do not break through nor steal. (Matthew 6:19–20)

This scripture reminds me of the humorous but instructive story of the wealthy, righteous man who pleaded with God to be able to take some of his wealth with him when he died. Finally one night an angel appeared and granted him his wish. He said he could take with him one briefcase and anything he could put into it. After much thought, the man reasoned that the item of greatest value for its size was gold. He sold what he needed to fill his briefcase with gold bullion bars. Finally, the day came. As his mortal body failed him, he had tied to his wrist his very heavy briefcase. When he died, true to the angel's words, he arrived on the other side with this suitcase still attached. "Well," said St. Peter, "this is unusual." The man explained about his request and the promise granted him. St. Peter replied, "Open it up. Let's see what valuable items you've brought." The man opened his brief case and St. Peter exclaimed in dismay, "Pavement? You've brought pavement?"

I see two morals to that story. First, those things that are valued in heaven are probably quite different than what we value here on earth. And second, the only things we can really take with us of value on the other side are those things that our spirit carries in its memory. Since wisdom and understanding were apparently highly valued before we came to earth see (Proverbs 8:23, 30), they will likely be held in high esteem hereafter as well. In fact Doctrine and Covenants 130:19 is quite explicit on that point: "And if a person gains more knowledge and intelligence in this life through his diligence and obedience than another, he will have so much the advantage in the world to come."

People who have had near-death experiences seem to validate this point. Those who have returned often affirm that mortal life is a time to learn, gain experience, and grow in knowledge and in wisdom.

I pray the principles, methods, and strategies that you have learned in this book will be of great value to you in that important endeavor. If you will apply them, I believe they will be of great value to you. I think you will be amazed at the many blessings you will enjoy as a result throughout your period of probation here on the earth and in the world to come. So keep at it, have fun, and may the Holy Spirit guide you and help you to remember.

For more practical tips and examples, go to chapter 12 under Additional Helps at www.ARECORD4LDS.com.

Notes:

1. See *The Screwtape Letters,* by C. S. Lewis for an interesting fictional, though insightful, treatise on how the devil and his demons work.

2. We could say that these evil enticements become purpose-defeating behaviors for them (the demons). If every time they try to tempt you, you respond with something uplifting, that defeats their purpose.

3. Richard W. Novacco, cited in the chapter on "Stress Inoculation" in Donald Meichenbaum, Cognitive-Behavior Modification: An Interactive Approach (New York: Plenum Press, 1977).

APPENDIX A

LEARNING STYLE SURVEY

Circle the letter before the response that seems to fit you best.

1. I seem to remember better ______.
    a. when I see things
    b. when I hear things

2. When listening to a lecture I sometimes like to ______.
    a. doodle
    b. focus on the nature of the words used

3. When attending a class, I would prefer the instructor ______.
   a. provide good visual aids
   b. explain in detail what he or she is talking about

4. When reading I find I can remember the material better if ______.
   a. I can visualize the events in my mind
   b. I read out loud

5. When learning about another country I would rather ______.
   a. see a movie showing different locations
   b. have someone tell me about the place or hear their music

6. When I try to remember things I find I do better when ______.
   a. I can visualize the setting where I learned the material
   b. I can remember hearing the information

7. I can memorize information better when ______.
   a. I can visualize the events or words on the page
   b. I recite the information over and over

If you selected "a" most often you are more visually inclined. If you selected more "b" responses then you may do better with more auditory or verbal methods of learning.

Circle your preference or fill in the blanks to help identify other learning preferences.

1. I concentrate better in the: morning—evening—other______

2. I prefer studying: alone—with a partner—in a group—combination.

3. I learn better when I am more: involved—relaxed.

4. I like to make: lists—draw pictures—create a collage.

5. I prefer studying when: it's quiet—I have soft music—
   I have music with a beat—other ________________

6. When I read I prefer: a bright room—a dim/cozy environment

7. When I study I prefer to: sit at a table—relax in a bean bag—
   Other ________________

Look at the elements you circled above. Then below design your ideal study environment, place, and time in accordance with your findings.

If I could create my ideal learning environment it would be as follows:

____

____

____

____

____

____

Unfortunately we cannot always have the ideal learning conditions, and we should be able to learn under most conditions. But if you follow your design, you may find you get a lot more out of your study time.

APPENDIX B

REMEMBERING THE BOOKS OF THE NEW TESTAMENT

In this section we will apply the link method to remembering the books of the New Testament, in order. This can be very useful when trying to look up passages. There are twenty-seven of them, so this will take a bit more time. But again I will get you started.

With this task I have used a different strategy. Most of the books have either the name of the author or the people to whom they were writing. Fortunately I have friends with the same names as the authors. You likely do as well—since Matthew, Mark, Luke, and John are four of the most common names in English.

So to remember the four gospels, I can just create a scene with my friends interacting. Actually, most students of the Bible won't have any problem remembering these first four books.

For an anchor I will place this interaction in the Seminary building where I first studied the New Testament. So I might imagine my four friends *Matt, Mark, Luke* and *John*, walking into the seminary building in that order. I see them enter the first room on the right. There I both see and hear them speak in different languages as they *Act* out a scene from the day of Pentecost. This of course is found in the book of Acts. Next I see a *Roman* soldier enter the room and tell them to cease such noise. He is eating two apples, and I see him throw their cores (*Corinthians*) into a trash can in the corner. Just then a young French cowgirl (gal—*Galatians*) comes into the room, and says to the Roman, "You can't just throw apple cores away here without paying eh fee, because we are ehfeesians (*Ephesians*)." So the Roman flips (*Philippians*) her a big shiny coin to pay his fee. "Fine," she says, "that closes (*Colossians*) the deal."

Do you see how easy that is? Note the story cue, or clue, doesn't have to be identical to the name, just close enough to remind you of it. Now it's your turn. I don't want to be having all the fun here. It may take some creative thinking to come up with something that reminds you of an unusual name, like Thessalonians, but with these, since we are not trying to remember actual scripture content, the more zany or unusual the images, the better. What word or name do you know that sounds like or would remind you of Thessalonians? I personally like the word *thistle*, but you may come up with something even better. Just remember, things that are concrete and easy to visualize are usually easiest to recall. This will be important for you to keep in mind, because whenever you're remembering things in sequence, whether it's books of the Bible, long passages of scripture or grocery items, the things in the middle are usually hardest to recall. So be sure and use some of the 10 Optimizing Strategies.

The following are the last fifteen books in the New Testament. I've included my symbols for reference, alongside the first few. But I suggest you use your own.

First Thessalonians (thistle)

Second Thessalonians

First Timothy (friend named Tim)

Second Timothy

Titus (Tide—on a beach or in a box in the laundry room.)

Philemon

Epistle to the Hebrews

Epistle of James

First Peter

Second Peter

First John

Second John

Third John

Jude

Revelation

This is not a difficult task. So if you are not already familiar with all the names and order of books in the New Testament, they won't be hard to learn. But it likely will take some effort and consistent rehearsal for a few days.

It's a good idea to review your major memory tasks just before going to bed, or even while in bed before you go to sleep. The brain seems to be able to store them more easily that way. One reason, of course, is that you then do not have other information coming in and "displacing" what you have just learned.

It's also helpful to add in some logical structural connections, or natural order if possible. For example, we know that after hearing the word (from the four **gospels**) it's important to **act** on those things we hear. So we have the "Acts" of the apostles. In Acts we hear of Paul who was a **Roman** citizen. It would seem only natural then that he would want to tell his fellow countrymen—the

Romans. We know he later sent epistles to others—the **Corinthians, Galatians, Ephesians, Philippians, Colossians, Thessalonians**—then to his former companion **Timothy**, as well as **Titus, Philemon**, and the **Hebrews**. Then we have letters from the first Presidency—**James, Peter** and **John** and finish up with **Jude** and John's **Revelation**.

SOURCES

Allen, James. *As A Man Thinketh.* Salt Lake City: Bookcraft, 2002.

Beck, Aaron T., Rush, A. J., Shaw, B. F., and Emery, G. *Cognitive Therapy of Depression.* New York: Gilford Press, 1979.

Burton, Rulon T., ed. *We Believe, Doctrines and Principles of The Church of Jesus Christ of Latter-day Saints.* Salt Lake City: Tabernacle Books, 1994.

Buzan, Tony. *The Mind Map Book: How to Use Radiant Thinking to Maximize Your Brain's Untapped Potential.* New York: Penguin Group, 1996.

Buzan, Tony. *Use Both Sides of Your Brain.* New York: Penguin Books, 1991.

Covey, Stephen R. *The Seven Habits of Highly Effective People.* New York: Simon & Schuster, 1989.

Crook, T. H. III and Adderly, B. *The Memory Cure.* New York: Simon & Schuster, 1998.

Dahl, L. and Cannon, D. *The Teachings of Joseph Smith.* Salt Lake City: Bookcraft, 1980.

Durham, G. Homer, ed. *Gospel Standards.* Salt Lake City: *Improvement Era*, 1941.

Gaskill, Alonzo. *The Lost Language of Symbolism.* Salt Lake City: Deseret Book, 2003.

Guidano, V. F. and Liotti, G. *Cognitive Processes and Emotional Disorders.* New York: Guilford Press, 1983.

Higbee, Kenneth L. *Your Memory, How It Works and How to Improve It.* New York: Marlowe & Company, 1996.

Householder, Leslie. *Heavenly Help with Money Matters.* Mesa, Ariz.: ThoughtsAlive Books, 2005.

Kimball, Edward L. ed. *The Teachings of Spencer W. Kimball.* Salt Lake City: Bookcraft, 1982.

Lapp, Danielle C. *Don't Forget.* Cambridge, Mass.: Perseus Books, 1995.

Lee, Harold B. *Stand Ye in Holy Places.* Salt Lake City: Deseret Book, 1974.

Leviton, Richard *Brain Builders: A Lifelong guide to sharper thinking, better memory, and an age proof mind.* Englewood Cliffs, N.J.: Prentice Hall, 1995.

Lewis, C. S. *The Screwtape Letters.* rev. ed. New York: Macmillan, 1982.

Ley, Beth M. *Marvelous Memory Boosters.* Temecula, Calif.: BL Publications, 2000.

Lombard Jay, and Germano, Carl. *The Brain Wellness Plan.* New York: Kensington Publishing Corp., 1997.

Ludlow, Victor L. *Isaiah: Prophet, Seer, and Poet.* Salt Lake City: Deseret Book, 1982.

Lyon, Jack M. et. al., eds. *Best-Loved Poems of the LDS People.* Salt Lake City: Deseret Book, 1996.

Madsen, Truman G. *How to Stop Forgetting and Start Remembering, a Practical Digest.* Provo, Utah: T. G. Madsen, 1968.

Maxwell, Neal A. *Sermons Not Spoken.* Salt Lake City: Bookcraft, 1985.

Meichenbaum, Donald. *Cognitive-Behavior Modification: An interactive Approach.* New York: Plenum Press, 1977.

Millet, Robert L. *Alive in Christ: The Miracle of Spiritual Rebirth.* Salt Lake City: Deseret Book, 1997.

Moody, Raymond. *The Light Beyond.* New York: Bantam Books, 1988.

Nelson, Aaron P. and Gilbert, Susan. *The Harvard Medical School Guide to Achieving Optimal Memory.* New York: McGraw-Hill, 2005.

Newquist, Jerreld L. ed. *George Q. Cannon Gospel Truth: Discourses and Writings of President George Q. Cannon.* Salt Lake City: Deseret Book, 1987.

Nibley, Hugh. *Since Cumorah.* Salt Lake City: Deseret Book, 1967.

Packer, Elder Boyd K. *Teach Ye Diligently*. Salt Lake City: Deseret Book Company, 1975.

Richards, R. D. and S. W. *Journal of Discourses*. Liverpool: R. D. Richards, 1854–1856.

Ring, Kenneth. *Lessons From The Light.* New York: Insight Books, 1998.

Sahelian, Ray M.D. *The Mind Boosters: Natural Supplements that Enhance Your Mind, Memory and Mood*. New York: St. Martin's Press, 2000.

Smith, Joseph Fielding. *Take Heed To Yourselves*. Salt Lake City: Deseret Book, 1971.

Talmage, James E. *Articles of Faith*. Salt Lake City: Deseret Book, 1984.

Teachings of Presidents of The Church. Salt Lake City: The Church of Jesus Christ of Latter-day Saints, 2004.

Valletta, Thomas R. Ed. *The New Testament for Latter-day Saint Families*. Salt Lake City: Bookcraft, 1998.

Watson, Elden J. *The Manuscript History of Brigham Young 1846–1847.* Salt Lake City: Elden J. Watson, 1971.

Welch, John W. *Chiasmus in Antiquity*. Provo, Utah: Brigham Young University, Research Press, 1981.

Whitaker, Julian. *The Memory Solution*. Garden City Park, N.Y.: Avery Publishing, 1999.

ABOUT THE AUTHOR

Born and raised on a family farm in Logan, Utah, David R. Larsen attended Utah State University on a track scholarship and majored in education.

Following a mission to Argentina, three years in the army, and his marriage in Switzerland to Maureen Kulinicz, of Coventry, England, he returned to the States to complete his bachelor's degree in psychology at the University of Utah. He later received a master's degree in family and human development from Utah State University.

For seven years, he served as a chaplain in the U.S. Navy and Marine Corps and then as a Family Life Programs manager for the Air Force. In his career he has taught numerous classes, in both the United States and Europe, on marriage and family relations, as well as on organizational and individual development. Recently, he served as director of the Organizational Health and Consulting Office at Hill Air Force Base, in Ogden, Utah. David also serves on the Utah board of the International Association for Near-Death Studies (IANDS) and is currently the director of Advanced Memory Dynamics.

David and Maureen live in Layton, Utah. They have two children and four grandchildren.

0 26575 79975 0